Desayu~~no (breakfast~~
almuer~~zo~~
cena (~~dinner~~

W9-CIL-198

Knife - cuchillo
fork - tenedor

sugar - azucar
egg - huevo
the bill - la cuenta
rare - poco hecho
medium - medio
well done - bien hecho

dessert - postres

towels - toalla
soap - jabon
shower - bano de ducha
room - cuarto or habitacion

Mae Caron

SPANISH
GRAMMAR
AND VERB TABLES

COLLINS
GEM

SPANISH GRAMMAR
AND VERB TABLES

A de Benito de Harland

In consultation with
I. F. Ariza

Collins
London and Glasgow

first published 1985

© William Collins Sons & Co. Ltd. 1985

latest reprint 1989

ISBN 0 00 459340 5

Editor
Jeremy M. Butterfield

Printed in Great Britain
Collins Clear-Type Press

INTRODUCTION

This book has been designed to help all learners of Spanish to get to grips with the grammar of the language, whatever stage you are at in learning Spanish. For beginners, the book provides a clear introduction to all the basic rules and structures, and more advanced learners will find it an invaluable guide for reference and revision.

For ease of use, each part of speech (nouns, verbs, adjectives etc) has been treated separately (see the list of contents on the next page). Wherever a grammatical term might be unfamiliar it has been explained or illustrated at the appropriate point in the text.

A special feature of this book is the clear demarcation of grammatical points, each treated on a left-hand page, and illustrated by examples in up-to-date Spanish on the opposite right-hand page. The eye is guided instantly to the appropriate example(s) by a system of bracketed numbers e.g. (→1), (→2) etc, corresponding to an example number on the facing page.

Special attention has been paid throughout to areas in which Spanish and English usage differ, thus helping the user to avoid the mistake of trying to translate English structures by identical structures in Spanish.

The tables of irregular verbs complement the extensive treatment of regular verbs in the grammar section of the book. In them 80 major irregular verbs are conjugated in their simple tenses so you can see where they differ from regular verbs. In addition, the verb index, in which all verbs are cross-referred to the appropriate conjugation model, enables you to check how over 2,800 Spanish verbs are conjugated.

A comprehensive index, containing key words in both Spanish and English, as well as subject references, completes the grammar.

Abbreviations used

algn.	alguien	**masc.**	masculine	**pres.**	present
ctd.	continued	**p(p).**	page(s)	**sb.**	somebody
cond.	conditional	**perf.**	perfect	**sing.**	singular
fem.	feminine	**pluperf.**	pluperfect	**sth.**	something
infin.	infinitive	**plur.**	plural	**subj.**	subjunctive

4 CONTENTS

CONTENTS 5

Simple Tenses: Formation

In Spanish the simple tenses are:

Present   (→1) ✓
Imperfect   (→2) ✓
Future   (→3) ✓
Conditional   (→4)
Preterite   (→5) ✓
Present Subjunctive (→6)
Imperfect Subjunctive (→7)

They are formed by adding endings to a verb stem. The endings show the number and person of the subject of the verb. (→8)

The stem and endings of regular verbs are totally predictable. The following sections show all the patterns for regular verbs. For irregular verbs see pp. 80 ff.

Regular Verbs

There are three regular verb patterns (called conjugations), each identifiable by the ending of the infinitive:

- First conjugation verbs end in **-ar** e.g. **hablar** to speak

- Second conjugation verbs end in **-er** e.g. **comer** to eat

- Third conjugation verbs end in **-ir** e.g. **vivir** to live

These three conjugations are treated in order on the following pages. The subject pronouns will appear in brackets because they are not always necessary in Spanish (see p. 226).

Continued

1 (yo) hablo
I speak, I am speaking, I do speak *(Present)*

2 (yo) hablaba
I spoke, I was speaking, I used to speak *Imperfect*

3 (yo) hablaré
I shall speak, I shall be speaking *Future*

4 (yo) hablaría
I should/would speak, I should/would be speaking *Cond.*

5 (yo) hablé
I spoke *Preterite - Simple Past.*

6 (que) (yo) hable
(that) I speak

7 (que) (yo) hablara or hablase
(that) I speak

8 (yo) hablo — I speak
(nosotros) hablamos — we speak
(yo) hablaría — I would speak
(nosotros) hablaríamos — we would speak

Simple Tenses: First Conjugation

● The stem is formed as follows:

TENSE	FORMATION	EXAMPLE
Present		
Imperfect		
Preterite	infinitive minus **-ar**	**habl-**
Present Subjunctive		
Imperfect Subjunctive		
Future	infinitive	**hablar-**
Conditional		

● To the appropriate stem add the following endings:

		PRESENT (→1)	IMPERFECT (→2)	PRETERITE (→3)
sing.	1st person	-o	-aba	-é
	2nd person	-as	-abas	-aste
	3rd person	-a	-aba	-ó
plur.	1st person	-amos	-ábamos	-amos
	2nd person	-áis	-abais	-asteis
	3rd person	-an	-aban	-aron

		PRESENT SUBJUNCTIVE (→4)	IMPERFECT SUBJUNCTIVE (→5)
sing.	1st person	-e	-ara or -ase
	2nd person	-es	-aras or -ases
	3rd person	-e	-ara or ase
plur.	1st person	-emos	-áramos or -ásemos
	2nd person	-éis	-arais or -aseis
	3rd person	-en	-aran or -asen

		FUTURE (→6)	CONDITIONAL (→7)
sing.	1st person	-é	-ía
	2nd person	-ás	-ías
	3rd person	-á	-ía
plur.	1st person	-emos	-íamos
	2nd person	-éis	-íais
	3rd person	-án	-ían

1 PRESENT

(yo)	hablo
(tú)	hablas
(él/ella)	habla
(Vd.)	habla
(nosotros/as)	hablamos
(vosotros/as)	habláis
(ellos/as)	hablan
(Vds.)	hablan

2 IMPERFECT

hablaba
hablabas
hablaba
hablaba
hablábamos
hablabais
hablaban
hablaban

3 PRETERITE

hablé
hablaste
habló
habló
hablamos
hablasteis
hablaron
hablaron

4 PRESENT SUBJUNCTIVE

(yo)	hable
(tú)	hables
(él/ella)	hable
(Vd.)	hable
(nosotros/as)	hablemos
(vosotros/as)	habléis
(ellos/as)	hablen
(Vds.)	hablen

5 IMPERFECT SUBJUNCTIVE

hablara or hablase
hablaras or hablases
hablara or hablase
hablara or hablase
habláramos or hablásemos
hablarais or hablaseis
hablaran or hablasen
hablaran or hablasen

6 FUTURE

(yo)	hablaré
(tú)	hablarás
(él/ella)	hablará
(Vd.)	hablará
(nosotros/as)	hablaremos
(vosotros/as)	hablaréis
(ellos/as)	hablarán
(Vds.)	hablarán

7 CONDITIONAL

hablaría
hablarías
hablaría
hablaría
hablaríamos
hablaríais
hablarían
hablarían

Simple Tenses: Second Conjugation

● The stem is formed as follows:

TENSE	FORMATION	EXAMPLE
Present		
Imperfect		
Preterite	infinitive minus -er	com-
Present Subjunctive		
Imperfect Subjunctive		
Future	infinitive	comer-
Conditional		

● To the appropriate stem add the following endings:

		PRESENT (→1)	IMPERFECT (→2)	PRETERITE (→3)
sing.	1st person	-o	-ía	-í
	2nd person	-es	-ías	-iste
	3rd person	-e	-ía	-ió
plur.	1st person	-emos	-íamos	-imos
	2nd person	-éis	-íais	-isteis
	3rd person	-en	-ían	-ieron

		PRESENT SUBJUNCTIVE (→4)	IMPERFECT SUBJUNCTIVE (→5)
sing.	1st person	-a	-iera or -iese
	2nd person	-as	-ieras or -ieses
	3rd person	-a	-iera or -iese
plur.	1st person	-amos	-iéramos or -iésemos
	2nd person	-áis	-ierais or -ieseis
	3rd person	-an	-ieran or -iesen

		FUTURE (→6)	CONDITIONAL (→7)
sing.	1st person	-é	-ía
	2nd person	-ás	-ías
	3rd person	-á	-ía
plur.	1st person	-emos	-íamos
	2nd person	-éis	-íais
	3rd person	-án	-ían

1 PRESENT

(yo)	como
(tú)	comes
(él/ella)	come
(Vd.)	come
(nosotros/as)	comemos
(vosotros/as)	coméis
(ellos/as)	comen
(Vds.)	comen

2 IMPERFECT

comía
comías
comía
comía
comíamos
comíais
comían
comían

3 PRETERITE

comí
comiste
comió
comió
comimos
comisteis
comieron
comieron

4 PRESENT SUBJUNCTIVE

(yo)	coma
(tú)	comas
(él/ella)	coma
(Vd.)	coma
(nosotros/as)	comamos
(vosotros/as)	comáis
(ellos/as)	coman
(Vds.)	coman

5 IMPERFECT SUBJUNCTIVE

comiera or comiese
comieras or comieses
comiera or comiese
comiera or comiese
comiéramos or comiésemos
comierais or comieseis
comieran or comiesen
comieran or comiesen

6 FUTURE

(yo)	comeré
(tú)	comerás
(él/ella)	comerá
(Vd.)	comerá
(nosotros/as)	comeremos
(vosotros/as)	comeréis
(ellos/as)	comerán
(Vds.)	comerán

7 CONDITIONAL

comería
comerías
comería
comería
comeríamos
comeríais
comerían
comerían

Simple Tenses: Third Conjugation

- The stem is formed as follows:

TENSE	FORMATION	EXAMPLE
Present		
Imperfect		
Preterite	infinitive minus -ir	viv-
Present Subjunctive		
Imperfect Subjunctive		
Future	infinitive	vivir-
Conditional		

- To the appropriate stem add the following endings:

		PRESENT (→1)	IMPERFECT (→2)	PRETERITE (→3)
sing.	1st person	-o	-ía	-í
	2nd person	-es	-ías	-iste
	3rd person	-e	-ía	-ió
plur.	1st person	-imos	-íamos	-imos
	2nd person	-ís	-íais	-isteis
	3rd person	-en	-ían	-ieron

		PRESENT SUBJUNCTIVE (→4)	IMPERFECT SUBJUNCTIVE (→5)
sing.	1st person	-a	-iera or -iese
	2nd person	-as	-ieras or -ieses
	3rd person	-a	-iera or -iese
plur.	1st person	-amos	-iéramos or -iésemos
	2nd person	-áis	-ierais or -ieseis
	3rd person	-an	-ieran or -iesen

		FUTURE (→6)	CONDITIONAL (→7)
sing.	1st person	-é	-ía
	2nd person	-ás	-ías
	3rd person	-á	-ía
plur.	1st person	-emos	-íamos
	2nd person	-éis	-íais
	3rd person	-án	-ían

1 PRESENT		**2** IMPERFECT	**3** PRETERITE
(yo)	vivo	vivía	viví
(tú)	vives	vivías	viviste
(él/ella)	vive	vivía	vivió
(Vd.)	vive	vivía	vivió
(nosotros/as)	vivimos	vivíamos	vivimos
(vosotros/as)	vivís	vivíais	vivisteis
(ellos/as)	viven	vivían	vivieron
(Vds.)	viven	vivían	vivieron

4 PRESENT SUBJUNCTIVE		**5** IMPERFECT SUBJUNCTIVE
(yo)	viva	viviera or viviese
(tú)	vivas	vivieras or vivieses
(él/ella)	viva	viviera or viviese
(Vd.)	viva	viviera or viviese
(nosotros/as)	vivamos	viviéramos or viviésemos
(vosotros/as)	viváis	vivierais or vivieseis
(ellos/as)	vivan	vivieran or viviesen
(Vds.)	vivan	vivieran or viviesen

6 FUTURE		**7** CONDITIONAL
(yo)	viviré	viviría
(tú)	vivirás	vivirías
(él/ella)	vivirá	viviría
(Vd.)	vivirá	viviría
(nosotros/as)	viviremos	viviríamos
(vosotros/as)	viviréis	viviríais
(ellos/as)	vivirán	vivirían
(Vds.)	vivirán	vivirían

The Imperative

The imperative is the form of the verb used to give commands or orders. It can be used politely, as in English 'Shut the door, please'.

In POSITIVE commands, the imperative forms for **Vd., Vds.** and **nosotros** are the same as the subjunctive. The other forms are as follows:

> **tú** (same as 3rd person singular present indicative)
> **vosotros** (final **-r** of infinitive changes to **-d**) (→1)

(tú)	**habla**	**come**	**vive**
	speak	*eat*	*live*
(Vd.)	**hable**	**coma**	**viva**
	speak	*eat*	*live*
(nosotros)	**hablemos**	**comamos**	**vivamos**
	let's speak	*let's eat*	*let's live*
(vosotros)	**hablad**	**comed**	**vivid**
	speak	*eat*	*live*
(Vds.)	**hablen**	**coman**	**vivan**
	speak	*eat*	*live*

In NEGATIVE commands, all the imperative forms are exactly the same as the present subjunctive.

- The imperative of irregular verbs is given in the verb tables, pp. 82 ff.

Position of object pronouns with the imperative

In POSITIVE commands: they follow the verb and are attached to it. An accent is needed to show the correct position for stress (see p. 292) (→2)
in NEGATIVE commands: they precede the verb and are not attached to it (→3)
- For the order of object pronouns, see page 232.

Continued

1 **cantar**   **cantad**
      to sing   sing

2 **Perdóneme**   **Enviémoselos**
      Excuse me   Let's send them to him/her/them
      Elíjanos   **Explíquemelo**
      Choose us   Explain it to me
      Esperémosla   **Devuélvaselo**
      Let's wait for her/it   Give it back to him/her/them

3 **No me molestes**   **No se la devolvamos**
      Don't disturb me   Let's not give it back to him/her/them
      No les castiguemos   **No me lo mandes**
      Let's not punish them   Don't send it to me
      No las conteste   **No nos lo hagan**
      Don't answer them   Don't do it to us

The Imperative (ctd.)

- For reflexive verbs — e.g. **levantarse** *to get up* — the object pronoun is the reflexive pronoun. It should be noted that the imperative forms need an accent to show the correct position for stress (see p. 292). The forms **nosotros** and **vosotros** also drop the final **-s** and **-d** respectively before the pronoun (→1) EXCEPTION: **idos** (**vosotros**) *go*

- Note: For general instructions, the infinitive is used instead of the imperative (→2), but when it is preceded by **vamos a** it often translates *let's . . .* (→3)

1 Levántate
Get up
Levántese (Vd.)
Get up
Levantémonos
Let's get up
Levantaos
Get up
Levántense (Vds.)
Get up

No te levantes
Don't get up
No se levante (Vd.)
Don't get up
No nos levantemos
Let's not get up
No os levantéis
Don't get up
No se levanten (Vds.)
Don't get up

2 Ver pág...
See page...
No pasar
Do not pass

3 Vamos a ver
Let's see
Vamos a empezar
Let's start

Compound Tenses: Formation

In Spanish the compound tenses are:

Perfect   (→1)
Pluperfect   (→2)
Future Perfect   (→3)
Conditional Perfect   (→4)
Past Anterior   (→5)
Perfect Subjunctive   (→6)
Pluperfect Subjunctive   (→7)

They consist of the past participle of the verb together with the auxiliary verb **haber**.

Compound tenses are formed in exactly the same way for both regular and irregular verbs, the only difference being that irregular verbs may have an irregular past participle.

The Past Participle

For all compound tenses you need to know how to form the past participle of the verb. For regular verbs this is as follows:

- 1st conjugation: replace the **-ar** of the infinitive by **-ado** (→8)
- 2nd conjugation: replace the **-er** of the infinitive by **-ido** (→9)
- 3rd conjugation: replace the **-ir** of the infinitive by **-ido** (→10)

Continued

1 **(yo) he hablado**
   I speak, I have spoken

2 **(yo) había hablado**
   I had spoken

3 **(yo) habré hablado**
   I shall have spoken

4 **(yo) habría hablado**
   I should/would have spoken

5 **(yo) hube hablado**
   I had spoken

6 **(que) (yo) haya hablado**
   (that) I spoke, have spoken

7 **(que) (yo) hubiera/hubiese hablado**
   (that) I had spoken

8 **cantar** → **cantado**
   to speak   spoken

9 **comer** → **comido**
   to eat   eaten

10 **vivir** → **vivido**
   to live   lived

Compound Tenses: formation (ctd.)

Perfect tense:	the present tense of **haber** plus the past participle (→**1**)
Pluperfect tense:	the imperfect tense of **haber** plus the past participle (→**2**)
Future Perfect:	the future tense of **haber** plus the past participle (→**3**)
Conditional Perfect:	the conditional of **haber** plus the past participle (→**4**)

Continued

1 PERFECT

(yo)	he hablado
(tú)	has hablado
(él/ella)	ha hablado
(Vd.)	ha hablado
(nosotros/as)	hemos hablado
(vosotros/as)	habéis hablado
(ellos/as)	han hablado
(Vds.)	han hablado

2 PLUPERFECT

(yo)	había hablado
(tú)	habías hablado
(él/ella)	había hablado
(Vd.)	había hablado
(nosotros/as)	habíamos hablado
(vosotros/as)	habíais hablado
(ellos/as)	habían hablado
(Vds.)	habían hablado

3 FUTURE PERFECT

(yo)	habré hablado
(tú)	habrás hablado
(él/ella)	habrá hablado
(Vd.)	habrá hablado
(nosotros/as)	habremos hablado
(vosotros/as)	habréis hablado
(ellos/as)	habrán hablado
(Vds.)	habrán hablado

4 CONDITIONAL PERFECT

(yo)	habría hablado
(tú)	habrías hablado
(él/ella)	habría hablado
(Vd.)	habría hablado
(nosotros/as)	habríamos hablado
(vosotros/as)	habríais hablado
(ellos/as)	habrían hablado
(Vds.)	habrían hablado

Compound Tenses (ctd.)

Past Anterior: the preterite of **haber** plus the past
                        participle (→**1**)

Perfect Subjunctive: the present subjunctive of **haber** plus
                        the past participle (→**2**)

Pluperfect Subjunctive: the imperfect subjunctive of **haber** plus
                        the past participle (→**3**)

- For how to form the past participle of regular verbs see p. 18.
  The past participle of irregular verbs is given for each verb in
  the verb tables, pp. 82 to 161.

1 PAST ANTERIOR

(yo)	**hube hablado**
(tú)	**hubiste hablado**
(él/ella)	**hubo hablado**
(Vd.)	**hubo hablado**
(nosotros/as)	**hubimos hablado**
(vosotros/as)	**hubisteis hablado**
(ellos/as)	**hubieron hablado**
(Vds.)	**hubieron hablado**

2 PERFECT SUBJUNCTIVE

(yo)	**haya hablado**
(tú)	**hayas hablado**
(él/ella)	**haya hablado**
(Vd.)	**haya hablado**
(nosotros/as)	**hayamos hablado**
(vosotros/as)	**hayáis hablado**
(ellos/as)	**hayan hablado**
(Vds.)	**hayan hablado**

3 PLUPERFECT SUBJUNCTIVE

(yo)	**hubiera** or **hubiese hablado**
(tú)	**hubieras** or **hubieses hablado**
(él/ella)	**hubiera** or **hubiese hablado**
(Vd.)	**hubiera** or **hubiese hablado**
(nosotros/as)	**hubiéramos** or **hubiésemos hablado**
(vosotros/as)	**hubierais** or **hubieseis hablado**
(ellos/as)	**hubieran** or **hubiesen hablado**
(Vds.)	**hubieran** or **hubiesen hablado**

Reflexive Verbs

A reflexive verb is one accompanied by a reflexive pronoun. The infinitive of a reflexive verb ends with the pronoun **se**, which is added to the verb form e.g.

levantarse *to get up;* **lavarse** *to wash (oneself).*

The reflexive pronouns are:

PERSON	SINGULAR	PLURAL
1st	**me**	**nos**
2nd	**te**	**os**
3rd	**se**	**se**

- The reflexive pronoun 'reflects back' to the subject, but it is not always translated in English (→1)
  The plural pronouns are sometimes translated as *one another, each other* (the 'reciprocal' meaning) (→2)
  The reciprocal meaning may be emphasized by **el uno al otro/ la una a la otra** (**los unos a los otros/las unas a las otras**) (→3)

- Both simple and compound tenses of reflexive verbs are conjugated in exactly the same way as those of non-reflexive verbs, except that the reflexive pronoun is always used.
  The only irregularity is in the 1st and 2nd person plural of the affirmative imperative (see p. 16). A sample reflexive verb is conjugated in full on pp. 28 to 31.

Position of reflexive pronouns

- Except with the infinitive, gerund and positive commands the pronoun comes before the verb (→4)

- In the infinitive, gerund and positive commands, the pronoun follows the verb and is attached to it (but see also p. 228) (→5)

Continued

1 **Me visto**
I'm dressing (myself)
Nos lavamos
We're washing (ourselves)
Se levanta
He gets up

2 **Nos queremos**
We love each other
Se parecen
They resemble one another

3 **Se miraban el uno al otro**
They were looking at each other

4 **Me acuesto temprano**
I go to bed early
¿Cómo se llama Vd.?
What is your name?
No se ha despertado
He hasn't woken up
No te levantes
Don't get up

5 **Quiero irme**
I want to go away
Estoy levantándome
I am getting up
Siéntense
Sit down
Vámonos Vamos
Let's go

Reflexive Verbs (ctd.)

Some verbs have both a reflexive and non-reflexive form. When used reflexively, they have a different but closely related meaning, as shown in the following examples.

Some common examples are:

NON-REFLEXIVE	REFLEXIVE
acostar to put to bed	**acostarse** to go to bed
casar to marry (off)	**casarse** to get married
detener to stop	**detenerse** to come to a halt
dormir to sleep	**dormirse** to go to sleep
enfadar to annoy	**enfadarse** to get annoyed
hacer to make	**hacerse** to become
ir to go	**irse** to go away
lavar to wash	**lavarse** to get washed
levantar to raise	**levantarse** to get up
llamar to call	**llamarse** to be called
poner to put	**ponerse** to put on (clothing), to become
sentir to feel (an object)	**sentirse** to feel (sick, tired, etc)
vestir to dress (someone)	**vestirse** to get dressed
volver to return	**volverse** to turn round

- Some other verbs exist only in the reflexive:

arrepentirse to repent	**jactarse** to boast
atreverse to dare	**quejarse** to complain

- Some verbs are used reflexively or non-reflexively without any change of meaning:

subir to go up	**subirse** to go up
morir to die	**morirse** to die

- Often a reflexive verb can be used:
  - to avoid the passive (see p. 34) (→1)
  - in impersonal expressions (see p. 40) (→2)

Continued

1 **Se perdió la batalla**
  The battle was lost
  No se veían las casas
  The houses could not be seen

2 **Se dice que . . .**
  (It is said that) People say that . . .
  No se puede entrar
  You/One can't go in
  No se permite
  It is not allowed

Reflexive Verbs (ctd.)

Conjugation of: **lavarse** to wash oneself

I SIMPLE TENSES

PRESENT

(yo)	**me lavo**
(tú)	**te lavas**
(él/ella/Vd.)	**se lava**
(nosotros/as)	**nos lavamos**
(vosotros/as)	**os laváis**
(ellos/as/Vds.)	**se lavan**

IMPERFECT

(yo)	**me lavaba**
(tú)	**te lavabas**
(él/ella/Vd.)	**se lavaba**
(nosotros/as)	**nos lavábamos**
(vosotros/as)	**os lavabais**
(ellos/as/Vds.)	**se lavaban**

FUTURE

(yo)	**me lavaré**
(tú)	**te lavarás**
(él/ella/Vd.)	**se lavará**
(nosotros/as)	**nos lavaremos**
(vosotros/as)	**os lavaréis**
(ellos/as/Vds.)	**se lavarán**

CONDITIONAL

(yo)	**me lavaría**
(tú)	**te lavarías**
(él/ella/Vd.)	**se lavaría**
(nosotros/as)	**nos lavaríamos**
(vosotros/as)	**os lavaríais**
(ellos/as/Vds.)	**se lavarían**

Reflexive Verbs (ctd.)

Conjugation of: **lavarse** *to wash oneself*

I SIMPLE TENSES

PRETERITE

(yo)	**me lavé**
(tú)	**te lavaste**
(él/ella/Vd.)	**se lavó**
(nosotros/as)	**nos lavamos**
(vosotros/as)	**os lavasteis**
(ellos/as/Vds.)	**se lavaron**

PRESENT SUBJUNCTIVE

(yo)	**me lave**
(tú)	**te laves**
(él/ella/Vd.)	**se lave**
(nosotros/as)	**nos lavemos**
(vosotros/as)	**os lavéis**
(ellos/as/Vds.)	**se laven**

IMPERFECT SUBJUNCTIVE

(yo)	**me lavara** or **lavase**
(tú)	**te lavaras** or **lavases**
(él/ella/Vd.)	**se lavara** or **lavase**
(nosotros/as)	**nos laváramos** or **lavásemos**
(vosotros/as)	**os lavarais** or **lavaseis**
(él/ella/Vds.)	**se lavaran** or **lavasen**

Continued

Reflexive Verbs (ctd.)

Conjugation of: **lavarse** to wash oneself

II COMPOUND TENSES

PERFECT

(yo)	**me he lavado**
(tú)	**te has lavado**
(él/ella/Vd.)	**se ha lavado**
(nosotros/as)	**nos hemos lavado**
(vosotros/as)	**os habéis lavado**
(ellos/as/Vds.)	**se han lavado**

PLUPERFECT

(yo)	**me había lavado**
(tú)	**te habías lavado**
(él/ella/Vd.)	**se había lavado**
(nosotros/as)	**nos habíamos lavado**
(vosotros/as)	**os habíais lavado**
(ellos/as/Vds.)	**se habían lavado**

FUTURE PERFECT

(yo)	**me habré lavado**
(tú)	**te habrás lavado**
(él/ella/Vd.)	**se habrá lavado**
(nosotros/as)	**nos habremos lavado**
(vosotros/as)	**os habréis lavado**
(ellos/as/Vds.)	**se habrán lavado**

Reflexive Verbs (ctd.)

Conjugation of: **lavarse** to wash oneself

II COMPOUND TENSES

PAST ANTERIOR

(yo)	me hube lavado
(tú)	te hubiste lavado
(él/ella/Vd.)	se hubo lavado
(nosotros/as)	nos hubimos lavado
(vosotros/as)	os hubisteis lavado
(ellos/as/Vds.)	se hubieron lavado

PERFECT SUBJUNCTIVE

(yo)	me haya lavado
(tú)	te hayas lavado
(él/ella/Vd.)	se haya lavado
(nosotros/as)	nos hayamos lavado
(vosotros/as)	os hayáis lavado
(ellos/as/Vds.)	se hayan lavado

PLUPERFECT SUBJUNCTIVE

(yo)	me hubiera or hubiese lavado
(tú)	te hubieras or hubieses lavado
(él/ella/Vd.)	se hubiera or hubiese lavado
(nosotros/as)	nos hubiéramos or hubiésemos lavado
(vosotros/as)	os hubierais or hubieseis lavado
(ellos/as/Vds.)	se hubieran or hubiesen lavado

The Passive

In active sentences, the subject of a verb carries out the action of
that verb, but in passive sentences the subject receives the action.
Compare the following:

The car hit Jane (subject: *the car*)
Jane was hit by the car (subject: *Jane*)

- English uses the verb 'to be' with the past participle to form
  passive sentences. Spanish forms them in the same way, i.e.:
  a tense of **ser** + past participle
  The past participle agrees in number and gender with the
  subject (→**1**)

  A sample verb is conjugated in the passive voice on pp. 36 to
  39.

- In English, the word 'by' usually introduces the agent through
  which the action of a passive sentence is performed. In
  Spanish this agent is preceded by **por** (→**2**)

- The Passive voice is used much less frequently in Spanish
  than English. It is, however, often used in expressions where
  the identity of the agent is unknown or unimportant (→**3**)

Continued

1 **Pablo ha sido despedido**
   Paul has been sacked
   Su madre era muy admirada
   His mother was greatly admired
   Los niños serán castigados
   The children will be punished
   Las puertas habían sido cerradas
   The doors had been closed

2 **La casa fue diseñada por mi hermano**
   The house was designed by my brother

3 **La ciudad fue conquistada tras un largo asedio**
   The city was conquered after a long siege
   Ha sido declarado el Estado de Excepción
   A State of Emergency has been declared

The Passive (ctd.)

In English the indirect object in an active sentence can become the subject of the related passive sentence,

e.g. *His mother gave him the book* (indirect object: *him*)
He was given the book by his mother

This is not possible in Spanish. The indirect object remains as such, while the object of the active sentence becomes the subject of the passive sentence (→1)

Other ways to express a passive meaning

Since modern Spanish tends to avoid the passive, it uses various other constructions to replace it:

- If the agent (person or object performing the action) is known, the active is often preferred where English might prefer the passive (→2)

- The 3rd person plural of the active voice can be used. The meaning is equivalent to *they* + verb (→3)

- When the action of the sentence is performed on a person, the reflexive form of the verb can be used in the 3rd person singular, and the person becomes the object (→4)

- When the action is performed on a thing, this becomes the subject of the sentence and the verb is made reflexive, agreeing in number with the subject (→5)

Continued

1 **Su madre le regaló el libro**
   His mother gave him the book
   becomes
   El libro le fue regalado por su madre
   The book was given to him by his mother

2 **La policía interrogó al sospechoso**
   The police questioned the suspect
   rather than
   El sospechoso fue interrogado por la policía

3 **Usan demasiada publicidad en la televisión**
   Too much advertising is used on television

4 **Últimamente no se le/les ha visto mucho en público**
   He has/they have not been seen much in public recently

5 **Esta palabra ya no se usa**
   This word is no longer used
   Todos los libros se han vendido
   All the books have been sold

The Passive (ctd.)

Conjugation of: **ser amado** *to be loved*

PRESENT

(yo)	**soy amado(a)**
(tú)	**eres amado(a)**
(él/ella/Vd.)	**es amado(a)**
(nosotros/as)	**somos amado(a)s**
(vosotros/as)	**sois amado(a)s**
(ellos/as/Vds.)	**son amado(a)s**

IMPERFECT

(yo)	**era amado(a)**
(tú)	**eras amado(a)**
(él/ella/Vd.)	**era amado(a)**
(nosotros/as)	**éramos amado(a)s**
(vosotros/as)	**erais amado(a)s**
(ellos/as/Vds.)	**eran amado(a)s**

FUTURE

(yo)	**seré amado(a)**
(tú)	**serás amado(a)**
(él/ella/Vd.)	**será amado(a)**
(nosotros/as)	**seremos amado(a)s**
(vosotros/as)	**seréis amado(a)s**
(ellos/as/Vds.)	**serán amado(a)s**

CONDITIONAL

(yo)	**sería amado (a)**
(tú)	**serías amado(a)**
(él/ella/Vd.)	**sería amado(a)**
(nosotros/as)	**seríamos amado(a)s**
(vosotros/as)	**serías amado(a)s**
(ellos/as/Vds.)	**serían amado(a)s**

The Passive (ctd.)

Conjugation of: **ser amado** *to be loved*

PRETERITE

(yo)	**fui amado(a)**
(tú)	**fuiste amado(a)**
(él/ella/Vd.)	**fue amado(a)**
(nosotros/as)	**fuimos amado(a)s**
(vosotros/as)	**fuisteis amado(a)s**
(ellos/as/Vds.)	**fueron amado(a)s**

PRESENT SUBJUNCTIVE

(yo)	**sea amado(a)**
(tú)	**seas amado(a)**
(él/ella/Vd.)	**sea amado(a)**
(nosotros/as)	**seamos amado(a)s**
(vosotros/as)	**seáis amado(a)s**
(ellos/as/Vds.)	**sean amado(a)s**

IMPERFECT SUBJUNCTIVE

(yo)	**fuera** or **fuese amado(a)**
(tú)	**fueras** or **fueses amado(a)**
(él/ella/Vd.)	**fuera** or **fuese amado(a)**
(nosotros/as)	**fuéramos** or **fuésemos amado(a)s**
(vosotros/as)	**fuerais** or **fueseis amado(a)s**
(ellos/as/Vds.)	**fueran** or **fuesen amado(a)s**

Continued

The Passive (ctd.)

Conjugation of: **ser amado** *to be loved*

PERFECT

(yo)	he sido amado(a)
(tú)	has sido amado(a)
(él/ella/Vd.)	ha sido amado(a)
(nosotros/as)	hemos sido amado(a)s
(vosotros/as)	habéis sido amado(a)s
(ellos/as/Vds.)	han sido amado(a)s

PLUPERFECT

(yo)	había sido amado(a)
(tú)	habías sido amado(a)
(él/ella/Vd.)	había sido amado(a)
(nosotros/as)	habíamos sido amado(a)s
(vosotros/as)	habíais sido amado(a)s
(ellos/as/Vds.)	habían sido amado(a)s

FUTURE PERFECT

(yo)	habré sido amado(a)
(tú)	habrás sido amado(a)
(él/ella/Vd.)	habrá sido amado(a)
(nosotros/as)	habremos sido amado(a)s
(vosotros/as)	habréis sido amado(a)s
(ellos/as/Vds.)	habrán sido amado(a)s

CONDITIONAL PERFECT

(yo)	habría sido amado(a)
(tú)	habrías sido amado(a)
(él/ella/Vd.)	habría sido amado(a)
(nosotros/as)	habríamos sido amado(a)s
(vosotros/as)	habríais sido amado(a)s
(ellos/as/Vds.)	habrían sido amado(a)s

The Passive (ctd.)

Conjugation of: **ser amado** *to be loved*

PAST ANTERIOR

(yo)	hube sido amado(a)
(tú)	hubiste sido amado(a)
(él/ella/Vd.)	hubo sido amado(a)
(nosotros/as)	hubimos sido amado(a)s
(vosotros/as)	hubisteis sido amado(a)s
(ellos/as/Vds.)	hubieron sido amado(a)s

PERFECT SUBJUNCTIVE

(yo)	haya sido amado(a)
(tú)	hayas sido amado(a)
(él/ella/Vd.)	haya sido amado(a)
(nosotros/as)	hayamos sido amado(a)s
(vosotros/as)	hayáis sido amado(a)s
(ellos/as/Vds.)	hayan sido amado(a)s

PLUPERFECT SUBJUNCTIVE

(yo)	hubiera/-se sido amado(a)
(tú)	hubieras/-ses sido amado(a)
(él/ella/Vd.)	hubiera/-se sido amado(a)
(nosotros/as)	hubiéramos/-semos sido amado(a)s
(vosotros/as)	hubierais/-seis sido amado(a)s
(ellos/as/Vds.)	hubieran/-se sido amado(a)s

Impersonal Verbs

Impersonal verbs are used only in the infinitive, the gerund, and in the 3rd person (usually singular); unlike English, Spanish does not use the subject pronoun with impersonal verbs.
e.g. **llueve**
it's raining
es fácil decir que . . .
it's easy to say that . . .

The most common impersonal verbs are:

INFINITIVE	CONSTRUCTION	
amanecer	**amanece/está amaneciendo** *it's daybreak*	
anochecer	**anochece/está anocheciendo** *it's getting dark*	
granizar	**graniza/está granizando** *it's hailing*	
llover	**llueve/está lloviendo** *it's raining*	(→1)
lloviznar	**llovizna/está lloviznando** *it's drizzling*	
nevar	**nieva/está nevando** *it's snowing*	
tronar	**truena/está tronando** *it's thundering*	

Some reflexive verbs are also used impersonally.
The most common are:

INFINITIVE	CONSTRUCTION
creerse	**se cree que*** + indicative (→2) *it is thought that; people think that*
decirse	**se dice que*** + indicative (→3) *it is said that; people say that*

Continued

1 Llovía a cántaros
    It was raining cats and dogs
    Estaba nevando cuando salieron
    It was snowing when they left

2 Se cree que llegarán mañana
    It is thought they will arrive tomorrow

3 Se dice que ha sido el peor invierno en **50** años
    People say it's been the worst winter in **50** years

Impersonal Verbs (ctd.)

INFINITIVE	CONSTRUCTION
poderse	**se puede** + infinitive (→1)
	one/people can, it is possible to
tratarse de	**se trata de** + noun (→2)
	it's a question/matter of something,
	it's about something
	se trata de + infinitive (→3)
	it's a question/matter of doing; somebody
	must do
venderse	**se vende*** + noun (→4)
	to be sold; for sale

*The same meaning can be conveyed by the 3rd person plural of these verbs; **creen que, dicen que, venden.**

The following verbs are also commonly used in impersonal constructions:

INFINITIVE	CONSTRUCTION
bastar	**basta con** + infinitive (→5)
	it is enough to do
	basta con + noun (→6)
	something is enough, it only takes sth
faltar	**falta** + infinitive (→7)
	we still have to
haber	**hay** + noun (→8)
	there is/are
	hay que + infinitive (→9)
	one has to/we have to
hacer	**hace** + noun/adjective depicting weather/dark/light etc. (→10)
	it is
	hace + time expression + **que** + indicative (→11)
	somebody has done or been doing something since . . .
	hace + time expression + **que** + negative indicative (→12)
	it is . . . since

Continued

1 **Aquí se puede aparcar**
One can park here

2 **No se trata de dinero**
It isn't a question/matter of money

3 **Se trata de poner fin al asunto**
We must put an end to the matter

4 **Se vende coche**
Car for sale

5 **Basta con telefonear para reservar un asiento**
You need only phone to reserve a seat

6 **Basta con un error para que todo se estropee**
One single error is enough to ruin everything

7 **Aún falta cerrar las maletas**
We still have to close our suitcases

8 **Hay una habitación libre**
There is one spare room
No había cartas esta mañana
There were no letters this morning

9 **Hay que cerrar las puertas**
We have to shut the doors

10 **Hace calor/viento/sol**
It is hot/windy/sunny
Mañana hará bueno
It'll be nice (weather) tomorrow

11 **Hace seis meses que vivo/vivimos aquí**
I/we have lived or been living here for six months

12 **Hace tres años que no le veo**
It is three years since I last saw him

Impersonal Verbs (ctd.)

INFINITIVE	CONSTRUCTION
hacer falta	**hace falta** + noun object (+ indirect object) (→1)
	(somebody) needs something, something is necessary (to somebody)
	hace falta + infinitive (+ indirect object) (→2)
	it is necessary to do
	hace falta que + subjunctive (→3)
	it is necessary to do, somebody must do
parecer	**parece que** (+ indirect object) + indicative (→4)
	it seems/appears that
ser	**es/son** + time expression (→5)
	it is
	es + de día/noche (→6)
	it is
	es + adjective + infinitive (→7)
	it is
ser mejor	**es mejor** + infinitive (→8)
	it's better to do
	es mejor que + subjunctive (→9)
valer más	**más vale** + infinitive (→10)
	it's better to do
	más vale que + subjunctive (→11)
	it's better to do/that somebody does

1 **Hace falta valor para hacer eso**
   One needs courage to do that; Courage is needed to do that
   Me hace falta otro vaso más
   I need an extra glass
2 **Hace falta volver**
   It is necessary to return; We/I/You must return*
   Me hacía falta volver
   I had to return
3 **Hace falta que Vd. se vaya**
   You have to/must leave
4 **(Me) parece que estás equivocado**
   It seems (to me) you are wrong
5 **Son las tres y media**
   It is half past three
   Ya es primavera
   It is Spring now
6 **Era de noche cuando llegamos**
   It was night when we arrived
7 **Era inútil protestar**
   It was useless to complain
8 **Es mejor no decir nada**
   It's better to keep quiet
9 **Es mejor que lo pongas aquí**
   It's better if you/that you put it here
10 **Más vale prevenir que curar**
   Prevention is better than cure
11 **Más valdría que no fuéramos**
   It would be better if we didn't go/We'd better not go

*The translation here obviously depends on context

The Infinitive

The infinitive is the form of the verb found in dictionary entries meaning 'to . . .', e.g. **hablar** *to speak*, **vivir** *to live*.

The infinitive is used in the following ways:
● After a preposition (→**1**)

● As a verbal noun (→**2**)
   In this use the article may precede the infinitive, especially when the infinitive is the subject and begins the sentence (→**3**)

● As a dependent infinitive, in the following verbal constructions:
   —with no linking preposition (→**4**)
   —with the linking preposition **a** (→**5**)
     (see also p. 66)
   —with the linking preposition **de** (→**6**)
     (see also p. 66)
   —with the linking preposition **en** (→**7**)
     (see also p. 66)
   —with the linking preposition **con** (→**8**)
     (see also p. 66)
   —with the linking preposition **por** (→**9**)
     (see also p. 66)

● The following construction should also be noted:
   indefinite pronoun + **que** + infinitive (→**10**)

● The object pronouns generally follow the infinitive and are attached to it. For exceptions see p. 228.

Continued

1 Después de acabar el desayuno, salió de casa
After finishing her breakfast she went out
Al enterarse de lo ocurrido se puso furiosa
When she found out what had happened she was furious
Me hizo daño sin saberlo
She hurt me without her knowing

2 Su deporte preferido es montar a caballo
Her favourite sport is horse riding
Ver es creer
Seeing is believing

3 El viajar tanto me resulta cansado
I find so much travelling tiring

4 ¿Quiere Vd. esperar?
Would you like to wait?

5 Aprenderán pronto a nadar
They will soon learn to swim

6 Pronto dejará de llover
It'll stop raining soon

7 La comida tarda en hacerse
The meal is taking a long time to cook

8 Amenazó con denunciarles
He threatened to report them (to the police)

9 Comience Vd. por decirme su nombre
Please start by giving me your name

10 Tengo algo que decirte
I have something to tell you

The Infinitive (ctd.)

The verbs set out below are followed by the infinitive with no linking preposition.

- deber, poder, saber, querer and tener que (hay que in impersonal constructions) (→1)

- valer más, hacer falta: see Impersonal Verbs, p. 45

- verbs of seeing or hearing e.g. ver to see, oír to hear (→2)

- hacer (→3)

- dejar to let, allow (→3)

- The following common verbs:

aconsejar	to advise	(→4)
conseguir	to manage to	(→5)
decidir	to decide	
desear	to wish, want	(→6)
esperar	to hope	(→7)
evitar	to avoid	(→8)
impedir	to prevent	(→9)
intentar	to try	(→10)
lograr	to manage to	(→5)
necesitar	to need	(→11)
odiar	to hate	
olvidar	to forget	(→12)
pensar	to think	(→13)
preferir	to prefer	(→14)
procurar	to try	(→10)
prohibir	to forbid	(→15)
prometer	to promise	(→16)
proponer	to propose	(→17)

Continued

1 **¿Quiere Vd. esperar?**
Would you like to wait?
No puede venir
She can't come

2 **Nos ha visto llegar**   **Se les oye cantar**
She saw us arriving   You can hear them singing
3 **No me hagas reír**   **Déjeme pasar**
Don't make me laugh   Let me past

4 **Le aconsejamos dejarlo para mañana**
We advise you to leave it until tomorrow

5 **Aún no he conseguido/logrado entenderlo**
I still haven't managed to understand it

6 **No desea tener más hijos**
She doesn't want to have any more children

7 **Esperamos ir de vacaciones este verano**
We are hoping to go on holiday this summer

8 **Evite beber cuando conduce**
Avoid drinking and driving

9 **No pudo impedirle hablar**
He couldn't prevent him from speaking

10 **Intentamos/procuramos pasar desapercibidos**
We tried not to be noticed

11 **Necesitaba salir a la calle**
I/he/she needed to go out

12 **Olvidó dejar su dirección**
He/she forgot to leave his/her address

13 **¿Piensan venir por Navidad?**
Are you thinking of coming for Christmas?

14 **Preferiría elegirlo yo mismo**
I'd rather choose it myself

15 **Prohibió fumar a los alumnos**
He forbade the pupils to smoke

16 **Prometieron volver pronto**
They promised to come back soon

17 **Propongo salir cuanto antes**
I propose to leave as soon as possible

The Infinitive: Set Expressions

The following are set in Spanish with the meaning shown:

dejar caer	to drop	(→1)
hacer entrar	to show in	(→2)
hacer saber	to let know, make known	(→3)
hacer salir	to let out	(→4)
hacer venir	to send for	(→5)
ir(se) a buscar	to go for, go and get	(→6)
mandar hacer	to order	(→7)
mandar llamar	to send for	(→8)
oír decir que	to hear it said that	(→9)
oír hablar de	to hear of/about	(→10)
querer decir	to mean	(→11)

The Perfect Infinitive

- The perfect infinitive is formed using the auxiliary verb **haber** with the past participle of the verb (→12)

- The perfect infinitive is found:
  - following certain prepositions, especially **después de** after (→13)
  - following certain verbal constructions (→14)

1 **Al verlo, dejó caer lo que llevaba en las manos**
When he saw him he dropped what he was carrying

2 **Haz entrar a nuestros invitados**
Show our guests in

3 **Quiero hacerles saber que no serán bien recibidos**
I want to let them know that they won't be welcome

4 **Hágale salir, por favor**
Please let him out

5 **Le he hecho venir a Vd. porque ...**
I sent for you because ...

6 **Vete a buscar los guantes**
Go and get your gloves

7 **Me he mandado hacer un traje**
I have ordered a suit

8 **Mandaron llamar al médico**
They sent for the doctor

9 **He oído decir que está enfermo**
I've heard it said that he's ill

10 **No he oído hablar más de él**
I haven't heard anything more (said) of him

11 **¿Qué quiere decir eso?**
What does that mean?

12 **Haber terminado**   **Haberse vestido**
To have finished   To have got dressed

13 **Después de haber comprado el regalo, volvió a casa**
After buying/having bought the present, he went back home
Después de haber madrugado tanto, el taxi se retrasó
After she got up so early, the taxi arrived late

14 **perdonar a alguien por haber hecho**
to forgive somebody for doing/having done
dar las gracias a alguien por haber hecho
to thank somebody for doing/having done
pedir perdón por haber hecho
to be sorry for doing/having done

The Gerund

Formation

- 1st conjugation
  Replace the **-ar** of the infinitive by **-ando** (→**1**)

- 2nd conjugation
  Replace the **-er** of the infinitive by **-iendo** (→**2**)

- 3rd conjugation
  Replace the **-ir** of the infinitive by **-iendo** (→**3**)

- For irregular gerunds, see irregular verbs, p. 80 ff.

Uses

- After the verb **estar**, to form the continuous tenses (→**4**)

- After the verbs **seguir** and **continuar** to continue, and **ir** when meaning to happen gradually (→**5**)

- In time constructions, after **llevar** (→**6**)

- When the action in the main clause needs to be complemented by another action (→**7**)

- The position of object pronouns is the same as for the infinitive (see p. 46).

- The gerund is invariable and strictly verbal in sense.

The Present Participle

- It is formed by replacing the **-ar** of the infinitive of 1st conjugation verbs by **-ante**, and the **-er** and **-ir** of the 2nd and 3rd conjugations by **-iente** (→**8**)

- A very limited number of verbs have a present participle, which is either used as an adjective or a noun (→**9/10**)

1 **cantar**   → **cantando**
   to sing   singing

2 **temer**   → **temiendo**
   to fear   fearing

3 **partir**   → **partiendo**
   to leave   leaving

4 **Estoy escribiendo una carta**
   I am writing a letter
   Estaban esperándonos
   They were waiting for us

5 **Sigue viniendo todos los días**
   He/she is still coming every day
   Continuarán subiendo los precios
   Prices will continue to go up
   El ejército iba avanzando poco a poco
   The army was gradually advancing

6 **Lleva dos años estudiando inglés**
   He/she has been studying English for two years

7 **Pasamos el día tomando el sol en la playa**
   We spent the day sunbathing on the beach
   Iba cojeando
   He/she/I was limping
   Salieron corriendo
   They ran out

8 **cantar**   → **cantante**
   to sing   singing/singer
   pender   → **pendiente**
   to hang   hanging
   seguir   → **siguiente**
   to follow   following

9 **agua corriente**
   running water

10 **un estudiante**
   a student

Use of Tenses

The Present

- Unlike English, Spanish often uses the same verb form for the simple present (e.g. *I smoke, he reads, we live*) and the continuous present (e.g. *I am smoking, he is reading, we are living*) (→1)
- Normally, however, the continuous present is used to translate the English:
  estar haciendo   *to be doing* (→2)
- Spanish uses the present tense where English uses the perfect in the following cases:
  - with certain prepositions of time – notably **desde** *for/since* – when an action begun in the past is continued in the present (→3)
    Note, however, that the perfect can be used as in English when the verb is negative (→4)
  - in the construction **acabar de hacer** *to have just done* (→5)
- Like English, Spanish often uses the present where a future action is implied (→6)

The Future

The future is generally used as in English (→7), but note the following:
- Immediate future time is often expressed by means of the present tense of **ir + a** + infinitive (→8)
- When 'will' or 'shall' mean 'wish to', 'are willing to', **querer** is used (→9)

The Future Perfect

- Used as in English *shall/will have done* (→10)
- It can also express conjecture, usually about things in the recent past (→11)

Continued

1 **Fumo** I smoke OR I am smoking
Lee He reads OR He is reading
Vivimos We live OR We are living

2 **Está fumando**
He is smoking

3 **Pablo aprende a nadar desde hace seis meses**
Paul's been learning to swim for six months (*and still is*)
Estoy de pie desde las siete
I've been up since seven
¿Hace mucho que esperan?
Have you been waiting long?
Ya hace dos semanas que estamos aquí
That's two weeks we've been here (now)

4 **No se han visto desde hace meses**
They haven't seen each other for months

5 **Isabel acaba de salir**
Isabel has just left

6 **Mañana voy a Madrid**
I am going to Madrid tomorrow

7 **Lo haré mañana**
I'll do it tomorrow

8 **Te vas a caer si no tienes cuidado**
You'll fall if you're not careful
Va a perder el tren
He's going to miss the train
Va a llevar una media hora
It'll take about half an hour

9 **¿Me quieres esperar un momento, por favor?**
Will you wait for me a second, please?

10 **Lo habré acabado para mañana**
I will have finished it for tomorrow

11 **Ya habrán llegado a casa**
They must have arrived home by now

Use of Tenses (ctd.)

The Imperfect
- The imperfect describes:
  - an action (or state) in the past without definite limits in time (→1)
  - habitual action(s) in the past (often expressed in English by means of *would* or *used to*) (→2)
- Spanish uses the imperfect tense where English uses the pluperfect in the following cases:
  - with certain prepositions of time — notably **desde** *for/since* when an action begun in the remoter past was continued in the more recent past (→3)
    Note, however, that the pluperfect is used as in English when the verb is negative or the action has been completed (→4)
  - in the construction **acabar de hacer** *to have just done* (→5)
- Both the continuous and simple forms can be translated by the Spanish simple imperfect, but the continuous imperfect is used when the emphasis is on the fact that an action was going on at a precise moment in the past (→6)

The Perfect
- The perfect is generally used as in English (→7)

The Preterite
- The preterite generally corresponds to the English simple past in both written and spoken Spanish (→8)
  However, while English can use the simple past to describe habitual actions or settings, Spanish uses the imperfect (see above) (→9)

The Past Anterior
- This tense is only ever used in written, literary Spanish, to replace the pluperfect in time clauses where the verb in the main clause is in the preterite (→10)

1 **Todos mirábamos en silencio**
We were all watching in silence
Nuestras habitaciones daban a la playa
Our rooms overlooked the beach

2 **En su juventud se levantaba de madrugada**
In his youth he got up at dawn
Hablábamos sin parar durante horas
We would talk non-stop for hours on end
Mi hermano siempre me tomaba el pelo
My brother always used to tease me

3 **Vivíamos en Roma hacía dos años**
We had been living in Rome for two years (and still were)
Estaba enfermo desde 1968
He had been ill since 1968
Hacía mucho tiempo que salían juntos
They had been going out together for a long time

4 **Hacía un año que no le había visto**
I hadn't seen him for a year
Hacía una hora que había llegado
She had arrived an hour before

5 **Acababa de encontrármelos**
I had just met them

6 **Cuando llegué, todos estaban fumando**
When I arrived, they were all smoking

7 **Todavía no han salido**
They haven't come out yet

8 **Me desperté y salté de la cama**
I woke up and jumped out of bed

9 **Siempre iban en coche al trabajo**
They always travelled to work by car

10 **Apenas hubo acabado, cuando se oyeron unos golpes en la puerta**
She had scarcely finished when there was a knock at the door

The Subjunctive: when to use it

(For how to form the subjunctive see pp. 6 ff.)

- After verbs of:
  - 'wishing'
    querer que
    desear que } to wish that, want (→1)
  - 'emotion' (e.g. regret, surprise, shame, pleasure, etc.)
    sentir que   to be sorry that (→2)
    sorprender que   to be surprised that (→3)
    alegrarse de que   to be pleased that (→4)
  - 'asking' and 'advising'
    pedir que   to ask that (→5)
    aconsejar que   to advise that (→6)

  In all the above constructions, when the subject of the verbs in the main and subordinate clause is the same, the infinitive is used, and the conjunction **que** omitted (→7)
  - 'ordering', 'forbidding', 'allowing'
    mandar que*
    ordenar que* } to order that (→8)
    permitir que*
    dejar que* } to allow that (→9)
    prohibir que*   to forbid that (→10)
    impedir que*   to prevent that (→11)

  *With these verbs either the subjunctive or the infinitive is used (→12)

- Always after verbs expressing doubt or uncertainty, and verbs of opinion used negatively
  dudar que   to doubt that (→13)
  no creer que
  no pensar que } not to think that (→14)

Continued

1 **Queremos que esté contenta**
We want her to be happy (literally: We want that she is happy)
¿Desea Vd. que lo haga yo?
Do you want me to do it?

2 **Sentí mucho que no vinieran**
I was very sorry that they didn't come

3 **Nos sorprendió que no les vieran Vds.**
We were surprised you didn't see them

4 **Me alegro de que te gusten**
I'm pleased that you like them

5 **Solo les pedimos que tengan cuidado**
We're only asking you to take care

6 **Le aconsejé que no llegara tarde**
I advised him not to be late

7 **Quiero que lo termines pronto**
I want you to finish it soon
BUT
Quiero terminarlo pronto
I want to finish it soon

8 **Ha mandado que vuelvan**
He has ordered them to come back
Ordenó que fueran castigados
He ordered them to be punished

9 **No permitas que te tomen el pelo**
Don't let them pull your leg
No me dejó que la llevara a casa
She didn't allow me to take her home

10 **Te prohíbo que digas eso**
I forbid you to say that

11 **No les impido que vengan**
I am not preventing them from coming

12 **Les ordenó que salieran OR Les ordenó salir**
She ordered them to go out

13 **Dudo que lo sepan hacer**
I doubt they can do it

14 **No creo que sean tan listos**
I don't think they are as clever as that

The Subjunctive: when to use it (ctd.)

- In impersonal constructions which express necessity, possibility, etc.

  hace falta que $\left.\right\}$ it is necessary that (→1)
  es necesario que

  es posible que   it is possible that (→2)
  más vale que   it is better that (→3)
  es una lástima que   it is a pity that (→4)

  Note that in impersonal constructions which state a fact or express certainty the indicative is used when the impersonal verb is affirmative. When it is negative, the subjunctive is used (→5)

- After certain conjunctions

  para que $\left.\right\}$ so that (→6)
  a fin de que*

  como si   as if (→7)
  sin que*   without (→8)

  a condición de que* $\left.\right\}$ provided that,
  con tal (de) que*   on condition that (→9)
  siempre que

  a menos que $\left.\right\}$ unless (→10)
  a no ser que

  antes (de) que*   before (→11)
  no sea que   lest (→12)

  mientras (que) $\left.\right\}$ as long as (→13)
  siempre que

  (el) que   the fact that (→14)

*When the subject of both verbs is the same, the infinitive is used, and the final que is omitted (→8)

Continued

1 **Es necesario que les hable inmediatamente**
   I must speak to them right away (It's necessary that I . . .)

2 **Es posible que tengan razón**
   It's possible that they are right

3 **Más vale que se quede Vd. en su casa**
   It's better that you stay at home

4 **Es una lástima que haya perdido su perrito**
   It's a shame/pity that she has lost her puppy

5 **Es verdad que va a venir**
   It's true that he's coming
   BUT
   No es verdad que vayan a hacerlo
   It's not true that they are going to do it

6 **Átalas bien para que no se caigan**
   Tie them up tightly so that they won't fall

7 **Hablaba como si no creyera en sus propias palabras**
   He talked as if he didn't believe in his own words

8 **Salimos sin que nos vieran**
   We left without them seeing us
   BUT
   Me fui sin esperarla
   I went without waiting for her

9 **Lo haré con tal de que me cuentes todo lo que pasó**
   I'll do it provided you tell me all that happened

10 **Saldremos de paseo a menos que esté lloviendo**
   We'll go for a walk unless it's raining

11 **Avísale antes de que sea demasiado tarde**
   Warn him before it's too late

12 **Habla en voz baja, no sea que alguien nos oiga**
   Speak softly lest anyone hears us

13 **Eso no pasará mientras yo sea el jefe aquí**
   That won't happen as long as I am the boss here

14 **El que no me escribiera no me importaba demasiado**
   That fact that he didn't write didn't matter to me too much

The Subjunctive: when to use it (ctd.)

- After the conjunctions

  de modo que
  de forma que $\left.\right\}$ so that (indicating a purpose) (→1)
  de manera que

Note that when these conjunctions introduce a result and not a
purpose the subjunctive is not used (→2)

- In relative clauses with an antecedent which is:
  - negative (→3)
  - indefinite (→4)
  - non-specific (→5)

- In main clauses, to express a wish or exhortation. The verb
  may be preceded by expressions like ojalá or que (→6)

- In the si clause of conditions where the English sentence
  contains a conditional tense (→7)

- In set expressions (→8)

- In the following constructions which translate *however*:
  - por + adjective + subjunctive (→9)
  - por + adverb + subjunctive (→10)
  - por + mucho + subjunctive (→11)

Continued

1 **Vuélvanse de manera que les vea bien**
   Turn round so that I can see you properly

2 **No quieren hacerlo, de manera que tendré que hacerlo yo**
   They won't do it, so I'll have to do it myself

3 **No he encontrado a nadie que la conociera**
   I haven't met anyone who knows her
   No dijo nada que no supiéramos ya
   He/she didn't say anything we didn't already know

4 **Necesito alguien que sepa conducir**
   I need someone who can drive
   Busco algo que me distraiga
   I'm looking for something to take my mind off it

5 **Busca una casa que tenga calefacción central**
   He/she's looking for a house which has central heating
   (subjunctive used since such a house may or may not exist)
   El que lo haya visto tiene que decírmelo
   Anyone who has seen it must tell me
   (subjunctive used since it is not known who has seen it)

6 **¡Ojalá haga buen tiempo!**
   Let's hope the weather will be good!
   ¡Que te diviertas!
   Have a good time!

7 **Si fuéramos en coche llegaríamos a tiempo**
   If we went by car we'd be there in time

8 **Diga lo que diga . . .**   **Sea lo que sea . . .**
   Whatever he may say . . .   Be that as it may . . .
   Pase lo que pase . . .   **Sea como sea . . .**
   Come what may . . .   One way or another . . .

9 **Por cansado que esté, seguirá trabajando**
   No matter how/however tired he may be, he'll go on working

10 **Por lejos que viva, iremos a buscarle**
   No matter how/however far away he lives, we'll go and look for him

11 **Por mucho que lo intente, nunca lo conseguirá**
   No matter how/however hard he tries, he'll never succeed

The Subjunctive (ctd.)

Clauses taking either a subjunctive or an indicative

In certain constructions, a subjunctive is needed when the action refers to future events or hypothetical situations, whereas an indicative is used when stating a fact or experience (→1)

The commonest of these are:

- The conjunctions

cuando	when (→1)
en cuanto tan pronto como }	as soon as (→2)
después (de) que*	after (→3)
hasta que	until (→4)
mientras	while (→5)
siempre que	whenever (→6)
aunque	even though (→7)

all conjunctions and pronouns ending in -quiera (-ever) (→8)

*Note that if the subject of both verbs is the same, the subjunctive introduced by **después (de) que** may be replaced by **después de** + infinitive (→9)

Sequence of tenses in Subordinate Clauses

- If the verb in the main clause is in the present, future or imperative, the verb in the dependent clause will be in the present or perfect subjunctive (→10)

- If the verb in the main clause is in the conditional or any past tense, the verb in the dependent clause will be in the imperfect or pluperfect subjunctive (→11)

1 **Le aconsejé que oyera música cuando estuviera nervioso**
I advised him to listen to music when he felt nervous
Me gusta nadar cuando hace calor
I like to swim when it is warm

2 **Te devolveré el libro tan pronto como lo haya leído**
I'll give you back the book as soon as I have read it

3 **Te lo diré después de que te hayas sentado**
I'll tell you after you've sat down

4 **Quédate aquí hasta que volvamos**
Stay here until we come back

5 **No hablen en voz alta mientras estén ellos aquí**
Don't speak loudly while they are here

6 **Vuelvan por aquí siempre que quieran**
Come back whenever you wish to

7 **No le creeré aunque diga la verdad**
I won't believe him even if he tells the truth

8 **La encontraré dondequiera que esté**
I will find her wherever she might be

9 **Después de cenar nos fuimos al cine**
After dinner we went to the cinema

10 **Quiero que lo hagas** (*pres. + pres. subj.*)
I want you to do it
Temo que no haya venido (*pres. + perf. subj.*)
I fear he hasn't come (might not have come)
Iremos por aquí para que no nos vean (*future + pres. subj.*)
We'll go this way so that they won't see us

11 **Me gustaría que llegaras temprano** (*cond. + imperf. subj.*)
I'd like you to arrive early
Les pedí que me esperaran (*preterite + pres. subj.*)
I asked them to wait for me
Sentiría mucho que hubiese muerto (*cond. + pluperf. subj.*)
I would be very sorry if he were dead

Verbs governing a, de, con, en, por and para

The following lists (p. 66 to 73) contain common verbal constructions using the prepositions **a, de, con, en, por** and **para**.

Note the following abbreviations:

infin.	infinitive
perf. infin.	perfect infinitive*
algn	alguien
sb	somebody
sth	something

*For formation see p. 50

aburrirse de + infin.	to get bored with doing (→**1**)
acabar con algo/algn	to put an end to sth/finish with sb (→**2**)
acabar de* + infin.	to have just done (→**3**)
acabar por + infin.	to end up doing (→**4**)
acercarse a algo/algn	to approach sb/sth
acordarse de algo/algn/de + infin.	to remember sth/sb/doing (→**5**)
acostumbrarse a algo/algn/a + infin.	to get used to sth/sb/to doing (→**6**)
acusar a algn **de** algo/**de** + perf. infin.	to accuse sb of sth/of having done (→**7**)
advertir a algn **de** algo	to notify, warn sb about sth (→**8**)
aficionarse a algo/**a** + infin.	to grow fond of sth/of doing (→**9**)
alegrarse de algo/**de** + perf. infin.	to be glad about sth/of doing, having done (→**10**)
alejarse de algn/algo	to move away from sb/sth
amenazar a algn **con** algo/**con** + infin.	to threaten sb with sth/to do (→**11**)
animar a algn **a** + infin.	to encourage sb to do
apresurarse a + infin.	to hurry to do (→**12**)

*See also Use of Tenses, pp. 54 and 56

Continued

1 **Me aburría de no poder salir de casa**
  I used to get bored with not being able to leave the house

2 **Quiso acabar con su vida**
  He wanted to put an end to his life

3 **Acababan de llegar cuando . . .**
  They had just arrived when . . .

4 **El acusado acabó por confesarlo todo**
  The accused ended up by confessing everything

5 **Nos acordamos muy bien de aquellas vacaciones**
  We remember that holiday very well

6 **Me he acostumbrado a levantarme temprano**
  I've got used to getting up early

7 **Le acusó de haber mentido**
  She accused him of lying

8 **Advertí a mi amigo del peligro que corría**
  I warned my friend about the danger he was in

9 **Nos hemos aficionado a la música clásica**
  We've grown fond of classical music

10 **Me alegro de haberle conocido**
  I'm glad I met him

11 **Amenazó con denunciarles**
  He threatened to report them

12 **Se apresuraron a coger sitio**
  They hurried to find a seat

Verbs governing a, de, con, en, por and para (ctd.)

aprender a + infin.	to learn to do (→1)
aprovecharse de algo/algn	to take advantage of sth/sb
aproximarse a algn/algo	to approach sb/sth
asistir a algo	to attend sth, be at sth
asomarse a/por	to lean out of (→2)
asombrarse de + infin.	to be surprised at doing (→3)
atreverse a + infin.	to dare to do
avergonzarse de algo/algn/de + perf. infin.	to be ashamed of sth/sb/of doing, having done (→4)
ayudar a algn a + infin.	to help sb to do (→5)
bajarse de (+ place/vehicle)	to get off/out of (→6)
burlarse de algn	to make fun of sb
cansarse de algo/algn/de + infin.	to tire of sth/sb/of doing
carecer de algo	to lack sth (→7)
cargar de algo	to load with sth (→8)
casarse con algn	to get married to sb (→9)
cesar de + infin.	to stop doing
chocar con algo	to crash/bump into sth (→10)
comenzar a + infin.	to begin to do
comparar con algn/algo	to compare with sb/sth
consentir en + infin.	to agree to do
consistir en + infin.	to consist of doing (→11)
constar de algo	to consist of sth (→12)
contar con algn/algo	to rely on sb/sth (→13)
convenir en + infin.	to agree to do (→14)
darse cuenta de algo	to realise sth
dejar de + infin.	to stop doing (→15)
depender de algo/algn	to depend on sth/sb (→16)
despedirse de algn	to say goodbye to sb
dirigirse a + place	to head for
disponerse a + infin.	to get ready to do
empezar a + infin.	to begin to do
empezar por + infin.	to begin by doing (→17)

Continued

1 **Me gustaría aprender a nadar**
   I'd like to learn to swim

2 **No te asomes a la ventana**
   Don't lean out of the window

3 **Nos asombramos mucho de verles ahí**
   We were very surprised at seeing them there

4 **No me avergüenzo de haberlo hecho**
   I'm not ashamed of having done it

5 **Ayúdeme a llevar estas maletas**
   Help me to carry these cases

6 **Se bajó del coche**
   He got out of the car

7 **La casa carecía de jardín**
   The house lacked (did not have) a garden

8 **El carro iba cargado de paja**
   The cart was loaded with straw

9 **Se casó con Andrés**
   She married Andrew

10 **Enciende la luz, o chocarás con la puerta**
   Turn the light on, or you'll bump into the door

11 **Mi plan consistía en vigilarles de cerca**
   My plan consisted of keeping a close eye on them

12 **El examen consta de tres partes**
   The exam consists of three parts

13 **Cuento contigo para que me ayudes a hacerlo**
   I rely on you to help me do it

14 **Convinieron en reunirse al día siguiente**
   They agreed to meet the following day

15 **¿Quieres dejar de hablar?**
   Will you stop talking?

16 **No depende de mí**
   It doesn't depend on me

17 **Empieza por enterarte de lo que se trata**
   Begin by finding out what it is about

Verbs governing a, de, con, en, por and para (ctd.)

encontrarse con algn	to meet sb (by chance) (→1)
enfadarse con algn	to get annoyed with sb
enseñar a algn a + infin.	to teach sb how to (→2)
enterarse de algo	to find out about sth (→3)
entrar en (+ place)	to enter, go into
esperar a + infin.	to wait until doing (→4)
estar de acuerdo con algn/algo	to agree with sb/sth
fiarse de algn/algo	to trust sb/sth
fijarse en algo/algn	to notice sth/sb (→5)
gozar de algo	to enjoy sth (→6)
hablar con algn	to talk to sb (→7)
hacer caso a algn	to pay attention to sb
hartarse de algo/algn/de + infin.	to get fed up with sth/sb/with doing (→8)
interesarse por algo/algn	to be interested in sth/sb (→9)
invitar a algn a + infin.	to invite sb to do
jugar a (+ sports, games)	to play
luchar por algo/por + infin.	to fight, strive for/to do (→10)
llegar a (+ place)/a + infin.	to reach/to manage to do (→11)
llenar de algo	to fill with
negarse a + infin.	to refuse to do
obligar a algn a + infin.	to make sb do (→12)
ocuparse de algn/algo	to take care of sb/attend to sth
oler a algo	to smell of sth (→13)
olvidarse de algo/algn/de + infin.	to forget sth/sb/to do (→14)
oponerse a algo/a + infin.	to be opposed to sth/to doing
parecerse a algn/algo	to resemble sb/sth
pensar en algo/algn/en + infin.	to think about sth/sb/about doing (→15)
preguntar por algn	to ask for/about sb
preocuparse de or por algo/algn	to worry about sth/sb (→16)

Continued

1 **Me encontré con ella al entrar en el Banco**
I met her as I was entering the Bank

2 **Le estoy enseñando a nadar**
I am teaching him to swim

3 **¿Te has enterado del sitio adonde hay que ir?**
Have you found out where we have to go?

4 **Espera a saber lo que quiere antes de comprar el regalo**
Wait until you know what he wants before buying the present

5 **Me fijé en él cuando subía a su coche**
I noticed him when he was getting into his car

6 **Gozamos mucho del espectáculo**
We enjoyed the show very much

7 **¿Puedo hablar con Vd. un momento?**
May I talk to you for a moment?

8 **Me he hartado de escribirle**
I've got fed up with writing to him

9 **Me interesaba mucho por la arqueología**
I was very interested in Archaeology

10 **Hay que luchar por mantener la paz**
One must strive to preserve peace

11 **Lo intenté sin llegar a conseguirlo**
I tried without managing to do it

12 **Le obligó a sentarse**
He made him sit down

13 **Este perfume huele a jazmín**
This perfume smells of jasmin

14 **Siempre me olvido de cerrar la puerta**
I always forget to shut the door

15 **No quiero pensar en eso**
I don't want to think about that

16 **Se preocupa mucho de/por su apariencia**
He worries a lot about his appearance

Verbs governing a, de, con, en, por and para (ctd.)

prepararse a + infin.	to prepare to do
probar a + infin.	to try to do
quedar en + infin.	to agree to do (→1)
quedar por + infin.	to remain to be done (→2)
quejarse de algo	to complain of sth
referirse a algo	to refer to sth
reírse de algo/algn	to laugh at sth/sb
rodear de	to surround with (→3)
romper a + infin.	to (suddenly) start to do (→4)
salir de (+ place)	to leave
sentarse a (+ table etc.)	to sit down at
subir(se) a (+ vehicle/place)	to get on, into/to climb (→5)
servir de algo a alguien	to serve/be useful to sb as sth (→6)
servir para algo/para + infin.	to be good as sth/for doing (→7)
servirse de algo	to use sth (→8)
soñar con algn/algo/con + infin.	to dream about/of sb/sth/of doing
sorprenderse de algo	to be surprised at sth
tardar en + infin.	to take time to do (→9)
tener ganas de algo/de + infin.	to want sth/to do (→10)
tener miedo de algo	to be afraid of sth (→11)
tener miedo a algn	to be afraid of sb (→12)
terminar por + infin.	to end by doing
tirar de algo/algn	to pull sth/sb
trabajar de (+ occupation)	to work as (→13)
trabajar en (+ place of work)	to work at/in (→14)
traducir a (+ language)	to translate into
tratar de + infin.	to try to do (→15)
tratarse de algo/algn/de + infin.	to be a question of sth/about sb/about doing (→16)
vacilar en + infin.	to hesitate to do (→17)
volver a + infin.	to do again (→18)

1 **Habíamos quedado en encontrarnos a las 8**
   We had agreed to meet at 8
2 **Queda por averiguar dónde se ocultan**
   It remains to be discovered where they are hiding
3 **Habían rodeado el jardín de un seto de cipreses**
   They had surrounded the garden with a hedge of cypress trees
4 **Al apagarse la luz, el niño rompió a llorar**
   When the lights went out, the little boy suddenly started to cry
5 **¡Deprisa, súbete al coche!**
   Get into the car, quick!
6 **Esto me servirá de bastón**
   This will serve me as a walking stick
7 **No sirvo para (ser) jardinero**
   I'm no good as a gardener
8 **Se sirvió de un destornillador para abrirlo**
   She used a screwdriver to open it
9 **Tardaron mucho en salir**
   They took a long time to come out
10 **Tengo ganas de volver a España**
   I want to go back to Spain
11 **Mi hija tiene miedo de la oscuridad**
   My daughter is afraid of the dark
12 **Nunca tuvieron miedo a su padre**
   They were never afraid of their father
13 **Pedro trabaja de camarero en Londres**
   Peter works as a waiter in London
14 **Trabajaba en una oficina**
   I used to work at an office
15 **No trates de engañarme**
   Don't try to fool me
16 **Se trata de nuestro nuevo vecino**
   It's about our new neighbour
17 **Nunca vacilaban en pedir dinero**
   They never hesitated to borrow money
18 **No vuelvas a hacerlo nunca más**
   Don't ever do it again

Ser and Estar

Spanish has two verbs — **ser** and **estar** — for *to be*.
They are not interchangeable and each one is used in defined contexts.

ser is used:

- With an adjective, to express a permanent or inherent quality (→1)
- To express occupation or nationality (→2)
- To express possession (→3)
- To express origin or the material from which something is made (→4)
- With a noun, pronoun or infinitive following the verb (→5)
- To express the time and date (→6)
- To form the passive, with the past participle (see p. 32). Note that this use emphasizes the action of the verb. If, however, the resultant state or condition needs to be emphasized, **estar** is used. The past participle then functions as an adjective (see p. 204) and has to agree in gender and in number with the noun (→7)

estar is used:

- Always, to indicate place or location (→8)
- With an adjective, to express a quality or state seen by the speaker as subject to change or different from expected (→9)
- When speaking of a person's state of health (→10)
- To form the continuous tenses, used with the gerund (see p. 52) (→11)
- With **de** + noun, to indicate a temporary occupation (→12)

Continued

1 **Mi hermano es alto**   **María es inteligente**
   My brother is tall   Mary is intelligent

2 **Javier es aviador**   **Sus padres son italianos**
   Javier is an airman   His parents are Italian

3 **La casa es de Miguel**
   The house belongs to Michael

4 **Mi hermana es de Granada**   **Las paredes son de ladrillo**
   My sister is from Granada   The walls are made of brick

5 **Andrés es un niño travieso**
   Andrew is a naughty boy
   Los cuadros son suyos
   The pictures are theirs
   Todo se proponérselo
   It's all a question of putting your mind to it

6 **Son las tres y media**   **Mañana es sábado**
   It's half past three   Tomorrow is Saturday

7 **Las puertas eran cerradas sigilosamente**
   The doors were being silently closed
   Las puertas estaban cerradas
   The doors were closed
   (resultant action)

8 **La comida está en la mesa**
   The meal is on the table

9 **Su amigo está enfermo**   **El lavabo está ocupado**
   Her friend is ill   The toilet is engaged
   Hoy estoy malhumorada   **Las tiendas están cerradas**
   I'm in a bad mood today   The shops are closed

10 **¿Cómo están Vds.?**   **Estamos todos bien**
   How are you?   We are all well

11 **Estamos aprendiendo mucho**
   We are learning a great deal

12 **Mi primo está de médico en un pueblo**
   My cousin works as a doctor in a village

Ser and Estar (ctd.)

With certain adjectives, both **ser** and **estar** can be used, although they are not interchangeable when used in this way:
— ser will express a permanent or inherent quality (→1)
— estar will express a temporary state or quality (→2)
Both ser and estar may also be used in set expressions.
The commonest of these are:

- With **ser**

Sea como sea	*Be that as it may*
Es igual/Es lo mismo	*It's all the same*
llegar a ser	*to become, turn out*
¿Cómo fue eso?	*How did that happen?*
¿Qué ha sido de él?	*What has become of him?*
ser para (with the idea of purpose)	*to be for* (→3)

- With **estar**

estar de pie/de rodillas	*to be standing/kneeling*
estar de viaje	*to be travelling*
estar de vacaciones	*to be on holiday*
estar de vuelta	*to be back*
estar de moda	*to be in fashion*
Está bien	*It's alright*
estar para	*to be about to do sth/to be in a mood for* (→4)
estar por	*to be inclined to/to be (all) for* (→5)
estar a punto de	*to be just about to do sth* (→6)

Continued

1   **Su hermana es muy joven/vieja**
His sister is very young/old
     Son muy ricos/pobres
They are very rich/poor
     Su amigo era un enfermo
His friend was an invalid
     Es un borracho
He is a drunkard
     Mi hijo es bueno/malo
My son is good/naughty
     Viajar es cansado
Travelling is tiring

2   **Está muy joven/vieja con ese vestido**
She looks very young/old in that dress
     Ahora están muy ricos/pobres
They have become very rich/poor lately
     Estaba enfermo
He was ill
     Está borracho
He is drunk
     Está bueno/malo
He is well/ill
     Hoy estoy cansada
I am tired today

3   **Este paquete es para Vd.**
This parcel is for you
     Esta caja es para guardar semillas
This box is for keeping seeds in

4   **Están para llegar**
They're about to arrive

5   **Estoy por irme a vivir a España**
I'm inclined to go and live in Spain

6   **Las rosas están a punto de salir**
The roses are about to come out

Verbal Idioms

Special Intransitive Verbs

With the following verbs the Spanish construction is the opposite of the English. The subject in English becomes the indirect object of the Spanish verb, while the object in English becomes the subject of the Spanish verb. Compare the following:

I like that house (subject: *I*, object: *that house*)

Esa casa me gusta (subject: **esa casa**, indirect object: **me**)

The commonest of these verbs are:

gustar	to like (→1)
gustar más	to prefer (→2)
encantar	(colloquial) to love (→3)
faltar	to need/to be short of/to have missing (→4)
quedar	to be/have left (→5)
doler	to have a pain in/to hurt, ache (→6)
interesar	to be interested in (→7)
importar	to mind (→8)

1 **Me gusta este vestido**
   I like this dress (This dress pleases me)

2 **Me gustan más éstas**
   I prefer these

3 **Nos encanta hacer deporte**
   We love sport

4 **Me faltaban 100 pesetas**
   I was short of 100 pesetas
   Sólo le falta el toque final
   It just needs the finishing touch
   Le faltaban tres dientes
   He/she had three teeth missing

5 **Sólo nos quedan dos kilómetros**
   We only have two kilometres (left) to go

6 **Me duele el pie izquierdo**
   I have a pain in my left foot (My left foot hurts)

7 **Nos interesa mucho la política**
   We are very interested in politics

8 **No me importa la lluvia**
   I don't mind the rain

Irregular Verbs

The verbs listed opposite and conjugated on pp. 82 to 161 provide the main patterns for irregular verbs. The verbs are grouped opposite according to their infinitive ending and are shown in the following tables in alphabetical order.

In the tables, the most important irregular verbs are given in their most common simple tenses, together with the imperative and the gerund.

The past participle is also shown for each verb, to enable you to form all the compound tenses, as on pp. 18 to 23.

- All the verbs included in the tables differ from the three conjugations set out on pp. 8 to 13. Many — e.g. **contar** — serve as models for groups of verbs, while others — e.g. **ir** — are unique. On pp. 162 to 186 you will find over 2,800 commonly used verbs listed alphabetically and cross referred either to the relevant basic conjugation or to the appropriate model in the verb tables.

'-ar':		'-er':	
	actuar		romper
	almorzar		saber
	andar		satisfacer
	aunar		tener
	avergonzar		torcer
	averiguar		traer
	contar		valer
	cruzar		vencer
	dar		ver
	empezar		volver
	enviar	'-ir':	abolir
	errar		abrir
	estar		adquirir
	jugar		bendecir
	negar		conducir
	pagar		construir
	pensar		cubrir
	rehusar		decir
	rogar		dirigir
	sacar		distinguir
	volcar		dormir
'-er':	caber		elegir
	caer		erguir
	cocer		escribir
	coger		freír
	crecer		gruñir
	entender		ir
	haber		lucir
	hay		morir
	hacer		oír
	leer		pedir
	llover		prohibir
	mover		reír
	nacer		reñir
	oler		reunir
	poder		salir
	poner		seguir
	querer		sentir
	resolver		venir
	ser		zurcir

abolir *to abolish*

PAST PARTICIPLE	IMPERATIVE
abolido	abolid

GERUND
aboliendo

PRESENT	PRESENT SUBJUNCTIVE
*	*not used*

| nosotros | abolimos |
| vosotros | abolís |

FUTURE		CONDITIONAL	
yo	aboliré	yo	aboliría
tú	abolirás	tú	abolirías
él	abolirá	él	aboliría
nosotros	aboliremos	nosotros	aboliríamos
vosotros	aboliréis	vosotros	aboliríais
ellos	abolirán	ellos	abolirían

IMPERFECT		PRETERITE	
yo	abolía	yo	abolí
tú	abolías	tú	aboliste
él	abolía	él	abolió
nosotros	abolíamos	nosotros	abolimos
vosotros	abolíais	vosotros	abolisteis
ellos	abolían	ellos	abolieron

*present tense only used in persons shown

abrir *to open*

PAST PARTICIPLE	IMPERATIVE
abierto	abre
	abrid

GERUND
abriendo

PRESENT

yo	abro
tú	abres
él	abre
nosotros	abrimos
vosotros	abrís
ellos	abren

FUTURE

yo	abriré
tú	abrirás
él	abrirá
nosotros	abriremos
vosotros	abriréis
ellos	abrirán

IMPERFECT

yo	abría
tú	abrías
él	abría
nosotros	abríamos
vosotros	abríais
ellos	abrían

PRESENT SUBJUNCTIVE

yo	abra
tú	abras
él	abra
nosotros	abramos
vosotros	abráis
ellos	abran

CONDITIONAL

yo	abriría
tú	abrirías
él	abriría
nosotros	abriríamos
vosotros	abriríais
ellos	abrirían

PRETERITE

yo	abrí
tú	abriste
él	abrió
nosotros	abrimos
vosotros	abristeis
ellos	abrieron

actuar *to act*

PAST PARTICIPLE
actuado

GERUND
actuando

IMPERATIVE
actúa
actuad

PRESENT		PRESENT SUBJUNCTIVE	
yo	actúo	yo	actúe
tú	actúas	tú	actúes
él	actúa	él	actúe
nosotros	actuamos	nosotros	actuemos
vosotros	actuáis	vosotros	actuéis
ellos	actúan	ellos	actúen

FUTURE		CONDITIONAL	
yo	actuaré	yo	actuaría
tú	actuarás	tú	actuarías
él	actuará	él	actuaría
nosotros	actuaremos	nosotros	actuaríamos
vosotros	actuaréis	vosotros	actuaríais
ellos	actuarán	ellos	actuarían

IMPERFECT		PRETERITE	
yo	actuaba	yo	actué
tú	actuabas	tú	actuaste
él	actuaba	él	actuó
nosotros	actuábamos	nosotros	actuamos
vosotros	actuabais	vosotros	actuasteis
ellos	actuaban	ellos	actuaron

adquirir *to acquire*

PAST PARTICIPLE
adquirido

IMPERATIVE
adquiere
adquirid

GERUND
adquiriendo

PRESENT
yo	**adquiero**
tú	**adquieres**
él	**adquiere**
nosotros	adquirimos
vosotros	adquirís
ellos	**adquieren**

PRESENT SUBJUNCTIVE
yo	**adquiera**
tú	**adquieras**
él	**adquiera**
nosotros	adquiramos
vosotros	adquiráis
ellos	**adquieran**

FUTURE
yo	adquiriré
tú	adquirirás
él	adquirirá
nosotros	adquiriremos
vosotros	adquiriréis
ellos	adquirirán

CONDITIONAL
yo	adquiriría
tú	adquirirías
él	adquiriría
nosotros	adquiriríamos
vosotros	adquiriríais
ellos	adquirirían

IMPERFECT
yo	adquiría
tú	adquirías
él	adquiría
nosotros	adquiríamos
vosotros	adquiríais
ellos	adquirían

PRETERITE
yo	adquirí
tú	adquiriste
él	adquirió
nosotros	adquirimos
vosotros	adquiristeis
ellos	adquirieron

almorzar to have lunch

PAST PARTICIPLE
almorzado

GERUND
almorzando

IMPERATIVE
almuerza
almorzad

PRESENT		PRESENT SUBJUNCTIVE	
yo	almuerzo	yo	almuerce
tú	almuerzas	tú	almuerces
él	almuerza	él	almuerce
nosotros	almorzamos	**nosotros**	**almorcemos**
vosotros	almorzáis	**vosotros**	**almorcéis**
ellos	**almuerzan**	ellos	almuercen

FUTURE		CONDITIONAL	
yo	almorzaré	yo	almorzaría
tú	almorzarás	tú	almorzarías
él	almorzará	él	almorzaría
nosotros	almorzaremos	nosotros	almorzaríamos
vosotros	almorzaréis	vosotros	almorzaríais
ellos	almorzarán	ellos	almorzarían

IMPERFECT		PRETERITE	
yo	almorzaba	**yo**	**almorcé**
tú	almorzabas	tú	almorzaste
él	almorzaba	él	almorzó
nosotros	almorzábamos	nosotros	almorzamos
vosotros	almorzabais	vosotros	almorzasteis
ellos	almorzaban	ellos	almorzaron

andar *to walk*

PAST PARTICIPLE
andado

IMPERATIVE
anda
andad

GERUND
andando

PRESENT		PRESENT SUBJUNCTIVE	
yo	ando	yo	ande
tú	andas	tú	andes
él	anda	él	ande
nosotros	andamos	nosotros	andemos
vosotros	andáis	vosotros	andéis
ellos	andan	ellos	anden

FUTURE		CONDITIONAL	
yo	andaré	yo	andaría
tú	andarás	tú	andarías
él	andará	él	andaría
nosotros	andaremos	nosotros	andaríamos
vosotros	andaréis	vosotros	andaríais
ellos	andarán	ellos	andarían

IMPERFECT		PRETERITE	
yo	andaba	yo	**anduve**
tú	andabas	tú	**anduviste**
él	andaba	él	**anduvo**
nosotros	andábamos	nosotros	**anduvimos**
vosotros	andabais	vosotros	**anduvisteis**
ellos	andaban	ellos	**anduvieron**

aunar *to join together*

PAST PARTICIPLE
aunado

IMPERATIVE
aúna
aunad

GERUND
aunando

PRESENT		PRESENT SUBJUNCTIVE	
yo	aúno	yo	aúne
tú	aúnas	tú	aúnes
él	aúna	él	aúne
nosotros	aunamos	nosotros	aunemos
vosotros	aunáis	vosotros	aunéis
ellos	aúnan	ellos	aúnen

FUTURE		CONDITIONAL	
yo	aunaré	yo	aunaría
tú	aunarás	tú	aunarías
él	aunará	él	aunaría
nosotros	aunaremos	nosotros	aunaríamos
vosotros	aunaréis	vosotros	aunaríais
ellos	aunarán	ellos	aunarían

IMPERFECT		PRETERITE	
yo	aunaba	yo	auné
tú	aunabas	tú	aunaste
él	aunaba	él	aunó
nosotros	aunábamos	nosotros	aunamos
vosotros	aunabais	vosotros	aunasteis
ellos	aunaban	ellos	aunaron

avergonzar *to shame*

PAST PARTICIPLE
avergonzado

GERUND
avergonzando

IMPERATIVE
avergüenza
avergonzad

PRESENT		PRESENT SUBJUNCTIVE	
yo	**avergüenzo**	yo	**avergüence**
tú	**avergüenzas**	tú	**avergüences**
él	**avergüenza**	él	**avergüence**
nosotros	avergonzamos	nosotros	**avergoncemos**
vosotros	avergonzáis	vosotros	**avergoncéis**
ellos	**avergüenzan**	ellos	**avergüencen**

FUTURE		CONDITIONAL	
yo	avergonzaré	yo	avergonzaría
tú	avergonzarás	tú	avergonzarías
él	avergonzará	él	avergonzaría
nosotros	avergonzaremos	nosotros	avergonzaríamos
vosotros	avergonzaréis	vosotros	avergonzaríais
ellos	avergonzarán	ellos	avergonzarían

IMPERFECT		PRETERITE	
yo	avergonzaba	yo	**avergoncé**
tú	avergonzabas	tú	avergonzaste
él	avergonzaba	él	avergonzó
nosotros	avergonzábamos	nosotros	avergonzamos
vosotros	avergonzabais	vosotros	avergonzasteis
ellos	avergonzaban	ellos	avergonzaron

averiguar to find out

PAST PARTICIPLE
averiguado

GERUND
averiguando

IMPERATIVE
averigua
averiguad

PRESENT
yo	averiguo
tú	averiguas
él	averigua
nosotros	averiguamos
vosotros	averiguáis
ellos	averiguan

PRESENT SUBJUNCTIVE
yo	**averigüe**
tú	**averigües**
él	**averigüe**
nosotros	**averigüemos**
vosotros	**averigüéis**
ellos	**averigüen**

FUTURE
yo	averiguaré
tú	averiguarás
él	averiguará
nosotros	averiguaremos
vosotros	averiguaréis
ellos	averiguarán

CONDITIONAL
yo	averiguaría
tú	averiguarías
él	averiguaría
nosotros	averiguaríamos
vosotros	averiguaríais
ellos	averiguarían

IMPERFECT
yo	averiguaba
tú	averiguabas
él	averiguaba
nosotros	averiguábamos
vosotros	averiguabais
ellos	averiguaban

PRETERITE
yo	**averigüé**
tú	averiguaste
él	averiguó
nosotros	averiguamos
vosotros	averiguasteis
ellos	averiguaron

bendecir *to bless*

PAST PARTICIPLE
bendecido

IMPERATIVE
bendice
bendecid

GERUND
bendiciendo

PRESENT
yo **bendigo**
tú **bendices**
él **bendice**
nosotros **bendecimos**
vosotros **bendecís**
ellos **bendicen**

PRESENT SUBJUNCTIVE
yo **bendiga**
tú **bendigas**
él **bendiga**
nosotros **bendigamos**
vosotros **bendigáis**
ellos **bendigan**

FUTURE
yo **bendeciré**
tú **bendecirás**
él **bendecirá**
nosotros **bendeciremos**
vosotros **bendeciréis**
ellos **bendecirán**

CONDITIONAL
yo **bendeciría**
tú **bendecirías**
él **bendeciría**
nosotros **bendeciríamos**
vosotros **bendeciríais**
ellos **bendecirían**

IMPERFECT
yo **bendecía**
tú **bendecías**
él **bendecía**
nosotros **bendecíamos**
vosotros **bendecíais**
ellos **bendecían**

PRETERITE
yo **bendije**
tú **bendijiste**
él **bendijo**
nosotros **bendijimos**
vosotros **bendijisteis**
ellos **bendijeron**

caber *to fit*

PAST PARTICIPLE
  cabido

IMPERATIVE
  cabe
  cabed

GERUND
  cabiendo

PRESENT		PRESENT SUBJUNCTIVE	
yo	quepo	yo	quepa
tú	cabes	tú	quepas
él	cabe	él	quepa
nosotros	cabemos	nosotros	quepamos
vosotros	cabéis	vosotros	quepáis
ellos	caben	ellos	quepan

FUTURE		CONDITIONAL	
yo	cabré	yo	cabría
tú	cabrás	tú	cabrías
él	cabrá	él	cabría
nosotros	cabremos	nosotros	cabríamos
vosotros	cabréis	vosotros	cabríais
ellos	cabrán	ellos	cabrían

IMPERFECT		PRETERITE	
yo	cabía	yo	cupe
tú	cabías	tú	cupiste
él	cabía	él	cupo
nosotros	cabíamos	nosotros	cupimos
vosotros	cabíais	vosotros	cupisteis
ellos	cabían	ellos	cupieron

caer *to fall*

PAST PARTICIPLE
caído

IMPERATIVE
cae
caed

GERUND
cayendo

PRESENT

yo	**caigo**
tú	caes
él	cae
nosotros	caemos
vosotros	caéis
ellos	caen

PRESENT SUBJUNCTIVE

yo	caiga
tú	caigas
él	caiga
nosotros	caigamos
vosotros	caigáis
ellos	caigan

FUTURE

yo	caeré
tú	caerás
él	caerá
nosotros	caeremos
vosotros	caeréis
ellos	caerán

CONDITIONAL

yo	caería
tú	caerías
él	caería
nosotros	caeríamos
vosotros	caeríais
ellos	caerían

IMPERFECT

yo	caía
tú	caías
él	caía
nosotros	caíamos
vosotros	caíais
ellos	caían

PRETERITE

yo	caí
tú	**caíste**
él	cayó
nosotros	**caímos**
vosotros	**caísteis**
ellos	**cayeron**

cocer *to boil*

PAST PARTICIPLE
cocido

IMPERATIVE
cuece
coced

GERUND
cociendo

PRESENT		PRESENT SUBJUNCTIVE	
yo	**cuezo**	yo	**cueza**
tú	**cueces**	tú	**cuezas**
él	**cuece**	él	**cueza**
nosotros	cocemos	**nosotros**	**cozamos**
vosotros	cocéis	**vosotros**	**cozáis**
ellos	**cuecen**	ellos	**cuezan**

FUTURE		CONDITIONAL	
yo	coceré	yo	cocería
tú	cocerás	tú	cocerías
él	cocerá	él	cocería
nosotros	coceremos	nosotros	coceríamos
vosotros	coceréis	vosotros	coceríais
ellos	cocerán	ellos	cocerían

IMPERFECT		PRETERITE	
yo	cocía	yo	cocí
tú	cocías	tú	cociste
él	cocía	él	coció
nosotros	cocíamos	nosotros	cocimos
vosotros	cocíais	vosotros	cocisteis
ellos	cocían	ellos	cocieron

coger *to catch*

PAST PARTICIPLE
  cogido

IMPERATIVE
  coge
  coged

GERUND
  cogiendo

PRESENT		PRESENT SUBJUNCTIVE	
yo	cojo	yo	coja
tú	coges	tú	cojas
él	coge	él	coja
nosotros	cogemos	nosotros	cojamos
vosotros	cogéis	vosotros	cojáis
ellos	cogen	ellos	cojan
FUTURE		CONDITIONAL	
yo	cogeré	yo	cogería
tú	cogerás	tú	cogerías
él	cogerá	él	cogería
nosotros	cogeremos	nosotros	cogeríamos
vosotros	cogeréis	vosotros	cogeríais
ellos	cogerán	ellos	cogerían
IMPERFECT		PRETERITE	
yo	cogía	yo	cogí
tú	cogías	tú	cogiste
él	cogía	él	cogió
nosotros	cogíamos	nosotros	cogimos
vosotros	cogíais	vosotros	cogisteis
ellos	cogían	ellos	cogieron

conducir *to drive, to lead*

PAST PARTICIPLE
conducido

IMPERATIVE
conduce
conducid

GERUND
conduciendo

PRESENT
yo **conduzco**
tú conduces
él conduce
nosotros conducimos
vosotros conducís
ellos conducen

PRESENT SUBJUNCTIVE
yo **conduzca**
tú **conduzcas**
él **conduzca**
nosotros **conduzcamos**
vosotros **conduzcáis**
ellos **conduzcan**

FUTURE
yo conduciré
tú conducirás
él conducirá
nosotros conduciremos
vosotros conduciréis
ellos conducirán

CONDITIONAL
yo conduciría
tú conducirías
él conduciría
nosotros conduciríamos
vosotros conduciríais
ellos conducirían

IMPERFECT
yo conducía
tú conducías
él conducía
nosotros conducíamos
vosotros conducíais
ellos conducían

PRETERITE
yo **conduje**
tú **condujiste**
él **condujo**
nosotros **condujimos**
vosotros **condujisteis**
ellos **condujeron**

construir *to build*

PAST PARTICIPLE
construido

IMPERATIVE
construye
construid

GERUND
construyendo

PRESENT

yo	construyo
tú	construyes
él	construye
nosotros	construimos
vosotros	construís
ellos	construyen

FUTURE

yo	construiré
tú	construirás
él	construirá
nosotros	construiremos
vosotros	construiréis
ellos	construirán

IMPERFECT

yo	construía
tú	construías
él	construía
nosotros	construíamos
vosotros	construíais
ellos	construían

PRESENT SUBJUNCTIVE

yo	construya
tú	construyas
él	construya
nosotros	construyamos
vosotros	construyáis
ellos	construyan

CONDITIONAL

yo	construiría
tú	construirías
él	construiría
nosotros	construiríamos
vosotros	construiríais
ellos	construirían

PRETERITE

yo	construí
tú	construiste
él	construyó
nosotros	construimos
vosotros	construisteis
ellos	construyeron

contar to tell, to count

PAST PARTICIPLE
contado

GERUND
contando

IMPERATIVE
cuenta
contad

PRESENT

yo	**cuento**
tú	**cuentas**
él	**cuenta**
nosotros	contamos
vosotros	contáis
ellos	**cuentan**

PRESENT SUBJUNCTIVE

yo	**cuente**
tú	**cuentes**
él	**cuente**
nosotros	contemos
vosotros	contéis
ellos	**cuenten**

FUTURE

yo	contaré
tú	contarás
él	contará
nosotros	contaremos
vosotros	contaréis
ellos	contarán

CONDITIONAL

yo	contaría
tú	contarías
él	contaría
nosotros	contaríamos
vosotros	contaríais
ellos	contarían

IMPERFECT

yo	contaba
tú	contabas
él	contaba
nosotros	contábamos
vosotros	contabais
ellos	contaban

PRETERITE

yo	conté
tú	contaste
él	contó
nosotros	contamos
vosotros	contasteis
ellos	contaron

crecer *to grow*

PAST PARTICIPLE
crecido

GERUND
creciendo

IMPERATIVE
crece
creced

PRESENT
yo	**crezco**
tú	creces
él	crece
nosotros	crecemos
vosotros	crecéis
ellos	crecen

FUTURE
yo	creceré
tú	crecerás
él	crecerá
nosotros	creceremos
vosotros	creceréis
ellos	crecerán

IMPERFECT
yo	crecía
tú	crecías
él	crecía
nosotros	crecíamos
vosotros	crecíais
ellos	crecían

PRESENT SUBJUNCTIVE
yo	**crezca**
tú	**crezcas**
él	**crezca**
nosotros	**crezcamos**
vosotros	**crezcáis**
ellos	**crezcan**

CONDITIONAL
yo	crecería
tú	crecerías
él	crecería
nosotros	creceríamos
vosotros	creceríais
ellos	crecerían

PRETERITE
yo	crecí
tú	creciste
él	creció
nosotros	crecimos
vosotros	crecisteis
ellos	crecieron

cruzar *to cross*

PAST PARTICIPLE
cruzado

IMPERATIVE
cruza
cruzad

GERUND
cruzando

PRESENT
yo cruzo
tú cruzas
él cruza
nosotros cruzamos
vosotros cruzáis
ellos cruzan

PRESENT SUBJUNCTIVE
yo cruce
tú cruces
él cruce
nosotros crucemos
vosotros crucéis
ellos crucen

FUTURE
yo cruzaré
tú cruzarás
él cruzará
nosotros cruzaremos
vosotros cruzaréis
ellos cruzarán

CONDITIONAL
yo cruzaría
tú cruzarías
él cruzaría
nosotros cruzaríamos
vosotros cruzaríais
ellos cruzarían

IMPERFECT
yo cruzaba
tú cruzabas
él cruzaba
nosotros cruzábamos
vosotros cruzabais
ellos cruzaban

PRETERITE
yo crucé
tú cruzaste
él cruzó
nosotros cruzamos
vosotros cruzasteis
ellos cruzaron

cubrir *to cover*

PAST PARTICIPLE
cubierto

IMPERATIVE
cubre
cubrid

GERUND
cubriendo

PRESENT	
yo	cubro
tú	cubres
él	cubre
nosotros	cubrimos
vosotros	cubrís
ellos	cubren

PRESENT SUBJUNCTIVE	
yo	cubra
tú	cubras
él	cubra
nosotros	cubramos
vosotros	cubráis
ellos	cubran

FUTURE	
yo	cubriré
tú	cubrirás
él	cubrirá
nosotros	cubriremos
vosotros	cubriréis
ellos	cubrirán

CONDITIONAL	
yo	cubriría
tú	cubrirías
él	cubriría
nosotros	cubriríamos
vosotros	cubriríais
ellos	cubrirían

IMPERFECT	
yo	cubría
tú	cubrías
él	cubría
nosotros	cubríamos
vosotros	cubríais
ellos	cubrían

PRETERITE	
yo	cubrí
tú	cubriste
él	cubrió
nosotros	cubrimos
vosotros	cubristeis
ellos	cubrieron

dar *to give*

PAST PARTICIPLE
  dado

IMPERATIVE
  da
  dad

GERUND
  dando

PRESENT		PRESENT SUBJUNCTIVE	
yo	doy	yo	dé
tú	das	tú	dés
él	da	él	dé
nosotros	damos	nosotros	demos
vosotros	dais	vosotros	deis
ellos	dan	ellos	den

FUTURE		CONDITIONAL	
yo	daré	yo	daría
tú	darás	tú	darías
él	dará	él	daría
nosotros	daremos	nosotros	daríamos
vosotros	daréis	vosotros	daríais
ellos	darán	ellos	darían

IMPERFECT		PRETERITE	
yo	daba	yo	di
tú	dabas	tú	diste
él	daba	él	dio
nosotros	dábamos	nosotros	dimos
vosotros	dabais	vosotros	disteis
ellos	daban	ellos	dieron

decir *to say*

PAST PARTICIPLE	IMPERATIVE
dicho	**di**
	decid

GERUND
diciendo

PRESENT		PRESENT SUBJUNCTIVE	
yo	**digo**	yo	**diga**
tú	**dices**	tú	**digas**
él	**dice**	él	**diga**
nosotros	**decimos**	nosotros	**digamos**
vosotros	**decís**	vosotros	**digáis**
ellos	**dicen**	ellos	**digan**

FUTURE		CONDITIONAL	
yo	**diré**	yo	**diría**
tú	**dirás**	tú	**dirías**
él	**dirá**	él	**diría**
nosotros	**diremos**	nosotros	**diríamos**
vosotros	**diréis**	vosotros	**diríais**
ellos	**dirán**	ellos	**dirían**

IMPERFECT		PRETERITE	
yo	**decía**	yo	**dije**
tú	**decías**	tú	**dijiste**
él	**decía**	él	**dijo**
nosotros	**decíamos**	nosotros	**dijimos**
vosotros	**decíais**	vosotros	**dijisteis**
ellos	**decían**	ellos	**dijeron**

dirigir to direct

PAST PARTICIPLE	IMPERATIVE
dirigido	dirige
	dirigid

GERUND
dirigiendo

PRESENT	PRESENT SUBJUNCTIVE
yo dirijo	yo dirija
tú diriges	tú dirijas
él dirige	él dirija
nosotros dirigimos	nosotros dirijamos
vosotros dirigís	vosotros dirijáis
ellos dirigen	ellos dirijan

FUTURE	CONDITIONAL
yo dirigiré	yo dirigiría
tú dirigirás	tú dirigirías
él dirigirá	él dirigiría
nosotros dirigiremos	nosotros dirigiríamos
vosotros dirigiréis	vosotros dirigiríais
ellos dirigirán	ellos dirigirían

IMPERFECT	PRETERITE
yo dirigía	yo dirigí
tú dirigías	tú dirigiste
él dirigía	él dirigió
nosotros dirigíamos	nosotros dirigimos
vosotros dirigíais	vosotros dirigisteis
ellos dirigían	ellos dirigieron

distinguir to distinguish

PAST PARTICIPLE
distinguido

IMPERATIVE
distingue
distinguid

GERUND
distinguiendo

PRESENT
yo distingo
tú distingues
él distingue
nosotros distinguimos
vosotros distinguís
ellos distinguen

PRESENT SUBJUNCTIVE
yo distinga
tú distingas
él distinga
nosotros distingamos
vosotros distingáis
ellos distingan

FUTURE
yo distinguiré
tú distinguirás
él distinguirá
nosotros distinguiremos
vosotros distinguiréis
ellos distinguirán

CONDITIONAL
yo distinguiría
tú distinguirías
él distinguiría
nosotros distinguiríamos
vosotros distinguiríais
ellos distinguirían

IMPERFECT
yo distinguía
tú distinguías
él distinguía
nosotros distinguíamos
vosotros distinguíais
ellos distinguían

PRETERITE
yo distinguí
tú distinguiste
él distinguió
nosotros distinguimos
vosotros distinguisteis
ellos distinguieron

dormir *to sleep*

PAST PARTICIPLE
dormido

IMPERATIVE
duerme
dormid

GERUND
durmiendo

PRESENT
yo	**duermo**
tú	**duermes**
él	**duerme**
nosotros	dormimos
vosotros	dormís
ellos	**duermen**

PRESENT SUBJUNCTIVE
yo	**duerma**
tú	**duermas**
él	**duerma**
nosotros	**durmamos**
vosotros	**durmáis**
ellos	**duerman**

FUTURE
yo	dormiré
tú	dormirás
él	dormirá
nosotros	dormiremos
vosotros	dormiréis
ellos	dormirán

CONDITIONAL
yo	dormiría
tú	dormirías
él	dormiría
nosotros	dormiríamos
vosotros	dormiríais
ellos	dormirían

IMPERFECT
yo	dormía
tú	dormías
él	dormía
nosotros	dormíamos
vosotros	dormíais
ellos	dormían

PRETERITE
yo	dormí
tú	dormiste
él	**durmió**
nosotros	dormimos
vosotros	dormisteis
ellos	**durmieron**

elegir *to choose*

PAST PARTICIPLE
elegido

GERUND
eligiendo

IMPERATIVE
elige
elegid

PRESENT		PRESENT SUBJUNCTIVE	
yo	elijo	yo	elija
tú	eliges	tú	elijas
él	elige	él	elija
nosotros	elegimos	nosotros	elijamos
vosotros	elegís	vosotros	elijáis
ellos	eligen	ellos	elijan

FUTURE		CONDITIONAL	
yo	elegiré	yo	elegiría
tú	elegirás	tú	elegirías
él	elegirá	él	elegiría
nosotros	elegiremos	nosotros	elegiríamos
vosotros	elegiréis	vosotros	elegiríais
ellos	elegirán	ellos	elegirían

IMPERFECT		PRETERITE	
yo	elegía	yo	elegí
tú	elegías	tú	elegiste
él	elegía	él	eligió
nosotros	elegíamos	nosotros	elegimos
vosotros	elegíais	vosotros	elegisteis
ellos	elegían	ellos	eligieron

empezar *to begin*

PAST PARTICIPLE
empezado

GERUND
empezando

IMPERATIVE
empieza
empezad

PRESENT
yo empiezo
tú empiezas
él empieza
nosotros empezamos
vosotros empezáis
ellos empiezan

FUTURE
yo empezaré
tú empezarás
él empezará
nosotros empezaremos
vosotros empezaréis
ellos empezarán

IMPERFECT
yo empezaba
tú empezabas
él empezaba
nosotros empezábamos
vosotros empezabais
ellos empezaban

PRESENT SUBJUNCTIVE
yo empiece
tú empieces
él empiece
nosotros empecemos
vosotros empecéis
ellos empiecen

CONDITIONAL
yo empezaría
tú empezarías
él empezaría
nosotros empezaríamos
vosotros empezaríais
ellos empezarían

PRETERITE
yo empecé
tú empezaste
él empezó
nosotros empezamos
vosotros empezasteis
ellos empezaron

entender *to understand*

PAST PARTICIPLE
entendido

IMPERATIVE
entiende
entended

GERUND
entendiendo

PRESENT
yo **entiendo**
tú **entiendes**
él **entiende**
nosotros entendemos
vosotros entendéis
ellos **entienden**

PRESENT SUBJUNCTIVE
yo **entienda**
tú **entiendas**
él **entienda**
nosotros entendamos
vosotros entendáis
ellos **entiendan**

FUTURE
yo entenderé
tú entenderás
él entenderá
nosotros entenderemos
vosotros entenderéis
ellos entenderán

CONDITIONAL
yo entendería
tú entenderías
él entendería
nosotros entenderíamos
vosotros entenderíais
ellos entenderían

IMPERFECT
yo entendía
tú entendías
él entendía
nosotros entendíamos
vosotros entendíais
ellos entendían

PRETERITE
yo entendí
tú entendiste
él entendió
nosotros entendimos
vosotros entendisteis
ellos entendieron

enviar *to send*

PAST PARTICIPLE
enviado

GERUND
enviando

IMPERATIVE
envía
enviad

PRESENT		PRESENT SUBJUNCTIVE	
yo	envío	yo	envíe
tú	envías	tú	envíes
él	envía	él	envíe
nosotros	enviamos	nosotros	enviemos
vosotros	enviáis	vosotros	enviéis
ellos	envían	ellos	envíen

FUTURE		CONDITIONAL	
yo	enviaré	yo	enviaría
tú	enviarás	tú	enviarías
él	enviará	él	enviaría
nosotros	enviaremos	nosotros	enviaríamos
vosotros	enviaréis	vosotros	enviaríais
ellos	enviarán	ellos	enviarían

IMPERFECT		PRETERITE	
yo	enviaba	yo	envié
tú	enviabas	tú	enviaste
él	enviaba	él	envió
nosotros	enviábamos	nosotros	enviamos
vosotros	enviabais	vosotros	enviasteis
ellos	enviaban	ellos	enviaron

erguir *to erect*

PAST PARTICIPLE
erguido

GERUND
irguiendo

IMPERATIVE
yergue
erguid

PRESENT		PRESENT SUBJUNCTIVE	
yo	**yergo**	yo	**yerga**
tú	**yergues**	tú	**yergas**
él	**yergue**	él	**yerga**
nosotros	**erguimos**	nosotros	**irgamos**
vosotros	**erguís**	vosotros	**irgáis**
ellos	**yerguen**	ellos	**yergan**

FUTURE		CONDITIONAL	
yo	**erguiré**	yo	**erguiría**
tú	**erguirás**	tú	**erguirías**
él	**erguirá**	él	**erguiría**
nosotros	**erguiremos**	nosotros	**erguiríamos**
vosotros	**erguiréis**	vosotros	**erguiríais**
ellos	**erguirán**	ellos	**erguirían**

IMPERFECT		PRETERITE	
yo	**erguía**	yo	**erguí**
tú	**erguías**	tú	**erguiste**
él	**erguía**	él	**irguió**
nosotros	**erguíamos**	nosotros	**erguimos**
vosotros	**erguíais**	vosotros	**erguisteis**
ellos	**erguían**	ellos	**irguieron**

errar *to err*

PAST PARTICIPLE
errado

IMPERATIVE
yerra
errad

GERUND
errando

PRESENT		PRESENT SUBJUNCTIVE	
yo	yerro	yo	yerre
tú	yerras	tú	yerres
él	yerra	él	yerre
nosotros	erramos	nosotros	erremos
vosotros	erráis	vosotros	erréis
ellos	yerran	ellos	yerren

FUTURE		CONDITIONAL	
yo	erraré	yo	erraría
tú	errarás	tú	errarías
él	errará	él	erraría
nosotros	erraremos	nosotros	erraríamos
vosotros	erraréis	vosotros	erraríais
ellos	errarán	ellos	errarían

IMPERFECT		PRETERITE	
yo	erraba	yo	erré
tú	errabas	tú	erraste
él	erraba	él	erró
nosotros	errábamos	nosotros	erramos
vosotros	errabais	vosotros	errasteis
ellos	erraban	ellos	erraron

escribir *to write*

PAST PARTICIPLE
escrito

GERUND
escribiendo

IMPERATIVE
escribe
escribid

PRESENT		PRESENT SUBJUNCTIVE	
yo	escribo	yo	escriba
tú	escribes	tú	escribas
él	escribe	él	escriba
nosotros	escribimos	nosotros	escribamos
vosotros	escribís	vosotros	escribáis
ellos	escriben	ellos	escriban

FUTURE		CONDITIONAL	
yo	escribiré	yo	escribiría
tú	escribirás	tú	escribirías
él	escribirá	él	escribiría
nosotros	escribiremos	nosotros	escribiríamos
vosotros	escribiréis	vosotros	escribiríais
ellos	escribirán	ellos	escribirían

IMPERFECT		PRETERITE	
yo	escribía	yo	escribí
tú	escribías	tú	escribiste
él	escribía	él	escribió
nosotros	escribíamos	nosotros	escribimos
vosotros	escribíais	vosotros	escribisteis
ellos	escribían	ellos	escribieron

estar *to be*

PAST PARTICIPLE	IMPERATIVE
estado	**está**
	estad

GERUND
estando

PRESENT		PRESENT SUBJUNCTIVE	
yo	estoy	yo	esté
tú	estás	tú	estés
él	está	él	esté
nosotros	estamos	nosotros	estemos
vosotros	estáis	vosotros	estéis
ellos	están	ellos	estén

FUTURE		CONDITIONAL	
yo	estaré	yo	estaría
tú	estarás	tú	estarías
él	estará	él	estaría
nosotros	estaremos	nosotros	estaríamos
vosotros	estaréis	vosotros	estaríais
ellos	estarán	ellos	estarían

IMPERFECT		PRETERITE	
yo	estaba	yo	estuve
tú	estabas	tú	estuviste
él	estaba	él	estuvo
nosotros	estábamos	nosotros	estuvimos
vosotros	estabais	vosotros	estuvisteis
ellos	estaban	ellos	estuvieron

freír *to fry*

PAST PARTICIPLE
frito

IMPERATIVE
fríe
freíd

GERUND
friendo

PRESENT
yo frío
tú fríes
él fríe
nosotros freímos
vosotros freís
ellos fríen

FUTURE
yo freiré
tú freirás
él freirá
nosotros freiremos
vosotros freiréis
ellos freirán

IMPERFECT
yo freía
tú freías
él freía
nosotros freíamos
vosotros freíais
ellos freían

PRESENT SUBJUNCTIVE
yo fría
tú frías
él fría
nosotros friamos
vosotros friáis
ellos frían

CONDITIONAL
yo freiría
tú freirías
él freiría
nosotros freiríamos
vosotros freiríais
ellos freirían

PRETERITE
yo freí
tú freíste
él frió
nosotros freímos
vosotros freísteis
ellos frieron

gruñir *to grunt*

PAST PARTICIPLE
gruñido

IMPERATIVE
gruñe
gruñid

GERUND
gruñendo

PRESENT

yo	gruño
tú	gruñes
él	gruñe
nosotros	gruñimos
vosotros	gruñís
ellos	gruñen

PRESENT SUBJUNCTIVE

yo	gruña
tú	gruñas
él	gruña
nosotros	gruñamos
vosotros	gruñáis
ellos	gruñan

FUTURE

yo	gruñiré
tú	gruñirás
él	gruñirá
nosotros	gruñiremos
vosotros	gruñiréis
ellos	gruñiran

CONDITIONAL

yo	gruñiría
tú	gruñirías
él	gruñiría
nosotros	gruñiríamos
vosotros	gruñiríais
ellos	gruñirían

IMPERFECT

yo	gruñía
tú	gruñías
él	gruñía
nosotros	gruñíamos
vosotros	gruñíais
ellos	gruñían

PRETERITE

yo	gruñi
tú	gruñiste
él	**gruño**
nosotros	gruñimos
vosotros	gruñisteis
ellos	**gruñeron**

haber to have (auxiliary)

PAST PARTICIPLE	IMPERATIVE
habido	*not used*

GERUND
habiendo

PRESENT		PRESENT SUBJUNCTIVE	
yo	he	yo	haya
tú	has	tú	hayas
él	ha	él	haya
nosotros	hemos	nosotros	hayamos
vosotros	habéis	vosotros	hayáis
ellos	han	ellos	hayan

FUTURE		CONDITIONAL	
yo	habré	yo	habría
tú	habrás	tú	habrías
él	habrá	él	habría
nosotros	habremos	nosotros	habríamos
vosotros	habréis	vosotros	habríais
ellos	habrán	ellos	habrían

IMPERFECT		PRETERITE	
yo	había	yo	hube
tú	habías	tú	hubiste
él	había	él	hubo
nosotros	habíamos	nosotros	hubimos
vosotros	habíais	vosotros	hubisteis
ellos	habían	ellos	hubieron

hacer *to do, to make*

PAST PARTICIPLE
hecho

IMPERATIVE
haz
haced

GERUND
haciendo

PRESENT	
yo	**hago**
tú	**haces**
él	**hace**
nosotros	**hacemos**
vosotros	**hacéis**
ellos	**hacen**

PRESENT SUBJUNCTIVE	
yo	**haga**
tú	**hagas**
él	**haga**
nosotros	**hagamos**
vosotros	**hagáis**
ellos	**hagan**

FUTURE	
yo	**haré**
tú	**harás**
él	**hará**
nosotros	**haremos**
vosotros	**haréis**
ellos	**harán**

CONDITIONAL	
yo	**haría**
tú	**harías**
él	**haría**
nosotros	**haríamos**
vosotros	**haríais**
ellos	**harían**

IMPERFECT	
yo	**hacía**
tú	**hacías**
él	**hacía**
nosotros	**hacíamos**
vosotros	**hacíais**
ellos	**hacían**

PRETERITE	
yo	**hice**
tú	**hiciste**
él	**hizo**
nosotros	**hicimos**
vosotros	**hicisteis**
ellos	**hicieron**

hay *there is, there are*

PAST PARTICIPLE
habido

IMPERATIVE
not used

GERUND
habiendo

PRESENT
hay

PRESENT SUBJUNCTIVE
haya

FUTURE
habrá

CONDITIONAL
habría

IMPERFECT
había

PRETERITE
hubo

ir *to go*

PAST PARTICIPLE
ido

IMPERATIVE
ve
id

GERUND
yendo

PRESENT		PRESENT SUBJUNCTIVE	
yo	voy	yo	vaya
tú	vas	tú	vayas
él	va	él	vaya
nosotros	vamos	nosotros	vayamos
vosotros	vais	vosotros	vayáis
ellos	van	ellos	vayan

FUTURE		CONDITIONAL	
yo	iré	yo	iría
tú	irás	tú	irías
él	irá	él	iría
nosotros	iremos	nosotros	iríamos
vosotros	iréis	vosotros	iríais
ellos	irán	ellos	irían

IMPERFECT		PRETERITE	
yo	iba	yo	fui
tú	ibas	tú	fuiste
él	iba	él	fue
nosotros	íbamos	nosotros	fuimos
vosotros	ibais	vosotros	fuisteis
ellos	iban	ellos	fueron

jugar *to play*

PAST PARTICIPLE
jugado

GERUND
jugando

IMPERATIVE
juega
jugad

PRESENT
yo **juego**
tú **juegas**
él **juega**
nosotros jugamos
vosotros jugáis
ellos **juegan**

PRESENT SUBJUNCTIVE
yo **juegue**
tú **juegues**
él **juegue**
nosotros **juguemos**
vosotros **juguéis**
ellos **jueguen**

FUTURE
yo jugaré
tú jugarás
él jugará
nosotros jugaremos
vosotros jugaréis
ellos jugarán

CONDITIONAL
yo jugaría
tú jugarías
él jugaría
nosotros jugaríamos
vosotros jugaríais
ellos jugarían

IMPERFECT
yo jugaba
tú jugabas
él jugaba
nosotros jugábamos
vosotros jugabais
ellos jugaban

PRETERITE
yo **jugué**
tú jugaste
él jugó
nosotros jugamos
vosotros jugasteis
ellos jugaron

leer *to read*

PAST PARTICIPLE	IMPERATIVE
leído	lee
	leed

GERUND
leyendo

PRESENT

yo	leo
tú	lees
él	lee
nosotros	leemos
vosotros	leéis
ellos	leen

FUTURE

yo	leeré
tú	leerás
él	leerá
nosotros	leeremos
vosotros	leeréis
ellos	leerán

IMPERFECT

yo	leía
tú	leías
él	leía
nosotros	leíamos
vosotros	leíais
ellos	leían

PRESENT SUBJUNCTIVE

yo	lea
tú	leas
él	lea
nosotros	leamos
vosotros	leáis
ellos	lean

CONDITIONAL

yo	leería
tú	leerías
él	leería
nosotros	leeríamos
vosotros	leeríais
ellos	leerían

PRETERITE

yo	leí
tú	leíste
él	leyó
nosotros	leímos
vosotros	leísteis
ellos	**leyeron**

lucir *to shine*

PAST PARTICIPLE
lucido

GERUND
luciendo

IMPERATIVE
luce
lucid

PRESENT
yo	luzco
tú	luces
él	luce
nosotros	lucimos
vosotros	lucís
ellos	lucen

PRESENT SUBJUNCTIVE
yo	luzca
tú	luzcas
él	luzca
nosotros	luzcamos
vosotros	luzcáis
ellos	luzcan

FUTURE
yo	luciré
tú	lucirás
él	lucirá
nosotros	luciremos
vosotros	luciréis
ellos	lucirán

CONDITIONAL
yo	luciría
tú	lucirías
él	luciría
nosotros	luciríamos
vosotros	luciríais
ellos	lucirían

IMPERFECT
yo	lucía
tú	lucías
él	lucía
nosotros	lucíamos
vosotros	lucíais
ellos	lucían

PRETERITE
yo	lucí
tú	luciste
él	lució
nosotros	lucimos
vosotros	lucisteis
ellos	lucieron

llover *to rain*

PAST PARTICIPLE llovido	IMPERATIVE *not used*
GERUND lloviendo	

PRESENT **llueve**	PRESENT SUBJUNCTIVE **llueva**
FUTURE lloverá	CONDITIONAL llovería
IMPERFECT llovía	PRETERITE llovió

morir *to die*

PAST PARTICIPLE
muerto

IMPERATIVE
muere
morid

GERUND
muriendo

PRESENT	
yo	**muero**
tú	**mueres**
él	**muere**
nosotros	**morimos**
vosotros	**morís**
ellos	**mueren**

PRESENT SUBJUNCTIVE	
yo	**muera**
tú	**mueras**
él	**muera**
nosotros	**muramos**
vosotros	**muráis**
ellos	**mueran**

FUTURE	
yo	**moriré**
tú	**morirás**
él	**morirá**
nosotros	**moriremos**
vosotros	**moriréis**
ellos	**morirán**

CONDITIONAL	
yo	**moriría**
tú	**morirías**
él	**moriría**
nosotros	**moriríamos**
vosotros	**moriríais**
ellos	**morirían**

IMPERFECT	
yo	**moría**
tú	**morías**
él	**moría**
nosotros	**moríamos**
vosotros	**moríais**
ellos	**morían**

PRETERITE	
yo	**morí**
tú	**moriste**
él	**murió**
nosotros	**morimos**
vosotros	**moristeis**
ellos	**murieron**

mover *to move*

PAST PARTICIPLE	IMPERATIVE
movido	**mueve**
	moved

GERUND
movviendo

GERUND
moviendo

PRESENT		PRESENT SUBJUNCTIVE	
yo	**muevo**	yo	**mueva**
tú	**mueves**	tú	**muevas**
él	**mueve**	él	**mueva**
nosotros	movemos	nosotros	movamos
vosotros	movéis	vosotros	mováis
ellos	**mueven**	ellos	**muevan**

FUTURE		CONDITIONAL	
yo	moveré	yo	movería
tú	moverás	tú	moverías
él	moverá	él	movería
nosotros	moveremos	nosotros	moveríamos
vosotros	moveréis	vosotros	moveríais
ellos	moverán	ellos	moverían

IMPERFECT		PRETERITE	
yo	movía	yo	moví
tú	movías	tú	moviste
él	movía	él	movió
nosotros	movíamos	nosotros	movimos
vosotros	movíais	vosotros	movisteis
ellos	movían	ellos	movieron

nacer *to be born*

PAST PARTICIPLE
nacido

IMPERATIVE
nace
naced

GERUND
naciendo

PRESENT		PRESENT SUBJUNCTIVE	
yo	nazco	yo	nazca
tú	naces	tú	nazcas
él	nace	él	nazca
nosotros	nacemos	nosotros	nazcamos
vosotros	nacéis	vosotros	nazcáis
ellos	nacen	ellos	nazcan

FUTURE		CONDITIONAL	
yo	naceré	yo	nacería
tú	nacerás	tú	nacerías
él	nacerá	él	nacería
nosotros	naceremos	nosotros	naceríamos
vosotros	naceréis	vosotros	naceríais
ellos	nacerán	ellos	nacerían

IMPERFECT		PRETERITE	
yo	nacía	yo	nací
tú	nacías	tú	naciste
él	nacía	él	nació
nosotros	nacíamos	nosotros	nacimos
vosotros	nacíais	vosotros	nacisteis
ellos	nacían	ellos	nacieron

negar *to deny*

PAST PARTICIPLE
negado

GERUND
negando

IMPERATIVE
niega
negad

PRESENT	
yo	**niego**
tú	**niegas**
él	**niega**
nosotros	negamos
vosotros	negáis
ellos	**niegan**

FUTURE	
yo	negaré
tú	negarás
él	negará
nosotros	negaremos
vosotros	negaréis
ellos	negarán

IMPERFECT	
yo	negaba
tú	negabas
él	negaba
nosotros	negábamos
vosotros	negabais
ellos	negaban

PRESENT SUBJUNCTIVE	
yo	**niegue**
tú	**niegues**
él	**niegue**
nosotros	**neguemos**
vosotros	**neguéis**
ellos	**nieguen**

CONDITIONAL	
yo	negaría
tú	negarías
él	negaría
nosotros	negaríamos
vosotros	negaríais
ellos	negarían

PRETERITE	
yo	**negué**
tú	negaste
él	negó
nosotros	negamos
vosotros	negasteis
ellos	negaron

oír *to hear*

PAST PARTICIPLE	IMPERATIVE
oído	**oye**
	oíd

GERUND
oyendo

PRESENT		PRESENT SUBJUNCTIVE	
yo	**oigo**	yo	**oiga**
tú	**oyes**	tú	**oigas**
él	**oye**	él	**oiga**
nosotros	**oímos**	nosotros	**oigamos**
vosotros	**oís**	vosotros	**oigáis**
ellos	**oyen**	ellos	**oigan**

FUTURE		CONDITIONAL	
yo	**oiré**	yo	**oiría**
tú	**oirás**	tú	**oirías**
él	**oirá**	él	**oiría**
nosotros	**oiremos**	nosotros	**oiríamos**
vosotros	**oiréis**	vosotros	**oiríais**
ellos	**oirán**	ellos	**oirían**

IMPERFECT		PRETERITE	
yo	**oía**	yo	**oí**
tú	**oías**	tú	**oíste**
él	**oía**	él	**oyó**
nosotros	**oíamos**	nosotros	**oímos**
vosotros	**oíais**	vosotros	**oísteis**
ellos	**oían**	ellos	**oyeron**

oler to smell

PAST PARTICIPLE
olido

IMPERATIVE
huele
oled

GERUND
oliendo

PRESENT		PRESENT SUBJUNCTIVE	
yo	**huelo**	yo	**huela**
tú	**hueles**	tú	**huelas**
él	**huele**	él	**huela**
nosotros	olemos	nosotros	olamos
vosotros	oléis	vosotros	oláis
ellos	**huelen**	**ellos**	**huelan**

FUTURE		CONDITIONAL	
yo	oleré	yo	olería
tú	olerás	tú	olerías
él	olerá	él	olería
nosotros	oleremos	nosotros	oleríamos
vosotros	oleréis	vosotros	oleríais
ellos	olerán	ellos	olerían

IMPERFECT		PRETERITE	
yo	olía	yo	olí
tú	olías	tú	oliste
él	olía	él	olió
nosotros	olíamos	nosotros	olimos
vosotros	olíais	vosotros	olisteis
ellos	olían	ellos	olieron

pagar *to pay*

PAST PARTICIPLE
pagado

IMPERATIVE
paga
pagad

GERUND
pagando

PRESENT
yo	pago
tú	pagas
él	paga
nosotros	pagamos
vosotros	pagáis
ellos	pagan

PRESENT SUBJUNCTIVE
yo	pague
tú	pagues
él	pague
nosotros	paguemos
vosotros	paguéis
ellos	paguen

FUTURE
yo	pagaré
tú	pagarás
él	pagará
nosotros	pagaremos
vosotros	pagaréis
ellos	pagarán

CONDITIONAL
yo	pagaría
tú	pagarías
él	pagaría
nosotros	pagaríamos
vosotros	pagaríais
ellos	pagarían

IMPERFECT
yo	pagaba
tú	pagabas
él	pagaba
nosotros	pagábamos
vosotros	pagabais
ellos	pagaban

PRETERITE
yo	pagué
tú	pagaste
él	pagó
nosotros	pagamos
vosotros	pagasteis
ellos	pagaron

pedir *to ask for*

PAST PARTICIPLE
  pedido

IMPERATIVE
  pide
  pedid

GERUND
  pidiendo

PRESENT
yo	pido
tú	pides
él	pide
nosotros	pedimos
vosotros	pedís
ellos	piden

PRESENT SUBJUNCTIVE
yo	pida
tú	pidas
él	pida
nosotros	pidamos
vosotros	pidáis
ellos	pidan

FUTURE
yo	pediré
tú	pedirás
él	pedirá
nosotros	pediremos
vosotros	pediréis
ellos	pedirán

CONDITIONAL
yo	pediría
tú	pedirías
él	pediría
nosotros	pediríamos
vosotros	pediríais
ellos	pedirían

IMPERFECT
yo	pedía
tú	pedías
él	pedía
nosotros	pedíamos
vosotros	pedíais
ellos	pedían

PRETERITE
yo	pedí
tú	pediste
él	pidió
nosotros	pedimos
vosotros	pedisteis
ellos	pidieron

pensar to think

PAST PARTICIPLE
pensado

IMPERATIVE
piensa
pensad

GERUND
pensando

PRESENT
yo **pienso**
tú **piensas**
él **piensa**
nosotros pensamos
vosotros pensáis
ellos **piensan**

PRESENT SUBJUNCTIVE
yo **piense**
tú **pienses**
él **piense**
nosotros pensemos
vosotros penséis
ellos **piensen**

FUTURE
yo pensaré
tú pensarás
él pensará
nosotros pensaremos
vosotros pensaréis
ellos pensarán

CONDITIONAL
yo pensaría
tú pensarías
él pensaría
nosotros pensaríamos
vosotros pensaríais
ellos pensarían

IMPERFECT
yo pensaba
tú pensabas
él pensaba
nosotros pensábamos
vosotros pensabais
ellos pensaban

PRETERITE
yo pensé
tú pensaste
él pensó
nosotros pensamos
vosotros pensasteis
ellos pensaron

poder *to be able*

PAST PARTICIPLE
podido

IMPERATIVE
puede
poded

GERUND
pudiendo

PRESENT
yo	**puedo**
tú	**puedes**
él	**puede**
nosotros	**podemos**
vosotros	**podéis**
ellos	**pueden**

PRESENT SUBJUNCTIVE
yo	**pueda**
tú	**puedas**
él	**pueda**
nosotros	**podamos**
vosotros	**podáis**
ellos	**puedan**

FUTURE
yo	**podré**
tú	**podrás**
él	**podrá**
nosotros	**podremos**
vosotros	**podréis**
ellos	**podrán**

CONDITIONAL
yo	**podría**
tú	**podrías**
él	**podría**
nosotros	**podríamos**
vosotros	**podríais**
ellos	**podrían**

IMPERFECT
yo	**podía**
tú	**podías**
él	**podía**
nosotros	**podíamos**
vosotros	**podíais**
ellos	**podían**

PRETERITE
yo	**pude**
tú	**pudiste**
él	**pudo**
nosotros	**pudimos**
vosotros	**pudisteis**
ellos	**pudieron**

poner *to put*

PAST PARTICIPLE	IMPERATIVE
puesto	**pon**
	poned

GERUND
poniendo

PRESENT		PRESENT SUBJUNCTIVE	
yo	**pongo**	yo	**ponga**
tú	**pones**	tú	**pongas**
él	**pone**	él	**ponga**
nosotros	**ponemos**	nosotros	**pongamos**
vosotros	**ponéis**	vosotros	**pongáis**
ellos	**ponen**	ellos	**pongan**

FUTURE		CONDITIONAL	
yo	**pondré**	yo	**pondría**
tú	**pondrás**	tú	**pondrías**
él	**pondrá**	él	**pondría**
nosotros	**pondremos**	nosotros	**pondríamos**
vosotros	**pondréis**	vosotros	**pondríais**
ellos	**pondrán**	ellos	**pondrían**

IMPERFECT		PRETERITE	
yo	**ponía**	yo	**puse**
tú	**ponías**	tú	**pusiste**
él	**ponía**	él	**puso**
nosotros	**poníamos**	nosotros	**pusimos**
vosotros	**poníais**	vosotros	**pusisteis**
ellos	**ponían**	ellos	**pusieron**

prohibir *to forbid*

PAST PARTICIPLE
prohibido

IMPERATIVE
prohíbe
prohibid

GERUND
prohibiendo

PRESENT		PRESENT SUBJUNCTIVE	
yo	prohíbo	yo	prohíba
tú	prohíbes	tú	prohíbas
él	prohíbe	él	prohíba
nosotros	prohibimos	nosotros	prohibamos
vosotros	prohibís	vosotros	prohibáis
ellos	prohíben	ellos	prohíban

FUTURE		CONDITIONAL	
yo	prohibiré	yo	prohibiría
tú	prohibirás	tú	prohibirías
él	prohibirá	él	prohibiría
nosotros	prohibiremos	nosotros	prohibiríamos
vosotros	prohibiréis	vosotros	prohibiríais
ellos	prohibirán	ellos	prohibirían

IMPERFECT		PRETERITE	
yo	prohibía	yo	prohibí
tú	prohibías	tú	prohibiste
él	prohibía	él	prohibió
nosotros	prohibíamos	nosotros	prohibimos
vosotros	prohibíais	vosotros	prohibisteis
ellos	prohibían	ellos	prohibieron

querer *to want*

PAST PARTICIPLE
querido

GERUND
queriendo

IMPERATIVE
quiere
quered

PRESENT	
yo	quiero
tú	quieres
él	quiere
nosotros	queremos
vosotros	queréis
ellos	quieren

PRESENT SUBJUNCTIVE	
yo	quiera
tú	quieras
él	quiera
nosotros	queramos
vosotros	queráis
ellos	quieran

FUTURE	
yo	querré
tú	querrás
él	querrá
nosotros	querremos
vosotros	querréis
ellos	querrán

CONDITIONAL	
yo	querría
tú	querrías
él	querría
nosotros	querríamos
vosotros	querríais
ellos	querrían

IMPERFECT	
yo	quería
tú	querías
él	quería
nosotros	queríamos
vosotros	queríais
ellos	querían

PRETERITE	
yo	quise
tú	quisiste
él	quiso
nosotros	quisimos
vosotros	quisisteis
ellos	quisieron

rehusar *to refuse*

PAST PARTICIPLE
rehusado

GERUND
rehusando

IMPERATIVE
rehúsa
rehusad

PRESENT
yo **rehúso**
tú **rehúsas**
él **rehúsa**
nosotros rehusamos
vosotros rehusáis
ellos **rehúsan**

PRESENT SUBJUNCTIVE
yo **rehúse**
tú **rehúses**
él **rehúse**
nosotros rehusemos
vosotros rehuséis
ellos **rehúsen**

FUTURE
yo rehusaré
tú rehusarás
él rehusará
nosotros rehusaremos
vosotros rehusaréis
ellos rehusarán

CONDITIONAL
yo rehusaría
tú rehusarías
él rehusaría
nosotros rehusaríamos
vosotros rehusaríais
ellos rehusarían

IMPERFECT
yo rehusaba
tú rehusabas
él rehusaba
nosotros rehusábamos
vosotros rehusabais
ellos rehusaban

PRETERITE
yo rehusé
tú rehusaste
él rehusó
nosotros rehusamos
vosotros rehusasteis
ellos rehusaron

reír to laugh

PAST PARTICIPLE
reído

GERUND
riendo

IMPERATIVE
ríe
reíd

PRESENT	
yo	río
tú	ríes
él	ríe
nosotros	reímos
vosotros	reís
ellos	ríen

PRESENT SUBJUNCTIVE	
yo	ría
tú	rías
él	ría
nosotros	riamos
vosotros	riáis
ellos	rían

FUTURE	
yo	reiré
tú	reirás
él	reirá
nosotros	reiremos
vosotros	reiréis
ellos	reirán

CONDITIONAL	
yo	reiría
tú	reirías
él	reiría
nosotros	reiríamos
vosotros	reiríais
ellos	reirían

IMPERFECT	
yo	reía
tú	reías
él	reía
nosotros	reíamos
vosotros	reíais
ellos	reían

PRETERITE	
yo	reí
tú	reíste
él	rio
nosotros	reímos
vosotros	reísteis
ellos	rieron

reñir to scold

PAST PARTICIPLE
reñido

GERUND
riñendo

IMPERATIVE
riñe
reñid

PRESENT		PRESENT SUBJUNCTIVE	
yo	riño	yo	riña
tú	riñes	tú	riñas
él	riñe	él	riña
nosotros	reñimos	nosotros	riñamos
vosotros	reñís	vosotros	riñáis
ellos	riñen	ellos	riñan

FUTURE		CONDITIONAL	
yo	reñiré	yo	reñiría
tú	reñirás	tú	reñirías
él	reñirá	él	reñiría
nosotros	reñiremos	nosotros	reñiríamos
vosotros	reñiréis	vosotros	reñiríais
ellos	reñirán	ellos	reñirían

IMPERFECT		PRETERITE	
yo	reñía	yo	reñí
tú	reñías	tú	reñiste
él	reñía	él	riñó
nosotros	reñíamos	nosotros	reñimos
vosotros	reñíais	vosotros	reñisteis
ellos	reñían	ellos	riñeron

resolver *to solve*

PAST PARTICIPLE
resuelto

GERUND
resolviendo

IMPERATIVE
resuelve
resolved

PRESENT

yo	**resuelvo**
tú	**resuelves**
él	**resuelve**
nosotros	resolvemos
vosotros	resolvéis
ellos	**resuelven**

FUTURE

yo	resolveré
tú	resolverás
él	resolverá
nosotros	resolveremos
vosotros	resolveréis
ellos	resolverán

IMPERFECT

yo	resolvía
tú	resolvías
él	resolvía
nosotros	resolvíamos
vosotros	resolvíais
ellos	resolvían

PRESENT SUBJUNCTIVE

yo	**resuelva**
tú	**resuelvas**
él	**resuelva**
nosotros	resolvamos
vosotros	resolváis
ellos	**resuelvan**

CONDITIONAL

yo	resolvería
tú	resolverías
él	resolvería
nosotros	resolveríamos
vosotros	resolveríais
ellos	resolverían

PRETERITE

yo	resolví
tú	resolviste
él	resolvió
nosotros	resolvimos
vosotros	resolvisteis
ellos	resolvieron

reunir to put together, gather

PAST PARTICIPLE	IMPERATIVE
reunido	**reúne**
	reunid

GERUND
reuniendo

PRESENT	PRESENT SUBJUNCTIVE
yo **reúno**	yo **reúna**
tú **reúnes**	tú **reúnas**
él **reúne**	él **reúna**
nosotros reunimos	nosotros reunamos
vosotros reunís	vosotros reunáis
ellos **reúnen**	ellos **reúnan**

FUTURE	CONDITIONAL
yo reuniré	yo reuniría
tú reunirás	tú reunirías
él reunirá	él reuniría
nosotros reuniremos	nosotros reuniríamos
vosotros reuniréis	vosotros reuniríais
ellos reunirán	ellos reunirían

IMPERFECT	PRETERITE
yo reunía	yo reuní
tú reunías	tú reuniste
él reunía	él reunió
nosotros reuníamos	nosotros reunimos
vosotros reuníais	vosotros reunisteis
ellos reunían	ellos reunieron

rogar *to beg*

PAST PARTICIPLE
rogado

IMPERATIVE
ruega
rogad

GERUND
rogando

PRESENT
yo **ruego**
tú **ruegas**
él **ruega**
nosotros rogamos
vosotros rogáis
ellos **ruegan**

PRESENT SUBJUNCTIVE
yo **ruegue**
tú **ruegues**
él **ruegue**
nosotros **roguemos**
vosotros **roguéis**
ellos **rueguen**

FUTURE
yo rogaré
tú rogarás
él rogará
nosotros rogaremos
vosotros rogaréis
ellos rogarán

CONDITIONAL
yo rogaría
tú rogarías
él rogaría
nosotros rogaríamos
vosotros rogaríais
ellos rogarían

IMPERFECT
yo rogaba
tú rogabas
él rogaba
nosotros rogábamos
vosotros rogabais
ellos rogaban

PRETERITE
yo **rogué**
tú rogaste
él rogó
nosotros rogamos
vosotros rogasteis
ellos rogaron

romper *to break*

PAST PARTICIPLE
roto

IMPERATIVE
rompe
romped

GERUND
rompiendo

PRESENT	
yo	rompo
tú	rompes
él	rompe
nosotros	rompemos
vosotros	rompéis
ellos	rompen

PRESENT SUBJUNCTIVE	
yo	rompa
tú	rompas
él	rompa
nosotros	rompamos
vosotros	rompáis
ellos	rompan

FUTURE	
yo	romperé
tú	romperás
él	romperá
nosotros	romperemos
vosotros	romperéis
ellos	romperán

CONDITIONAL	
yo	rompería
tú	romperías
él	rompería
nosotros	romperíamos
vosotros	romperíais
ellos	romperían

IMPERFECT	
yo	rompía
tú	rompías
él	rompía
nosotros	rompíamos
vosotros	rompíais
ellos	rompían

PRETERITE	
yo	rompí
tú	rompiste
él	rompió
nosotros	rompimos
vosotros	rompisteis
ellos	rompieron

saber *to know*

PAST PARTICIPLE	IMPERATIVE
sabido	sabe
	sabed

GERUND
sabiendo

PRESENT		PRESENT SUBJUNCTIVE	
yo	sé	yo	sepa
tú	sabes	tú	sepas
él	sabe	él	sepa
nosotros	sabemos	nosotros	sepamos
vosotros	sabéis	vosotros	sepáis
ellos	saben	ellos	sepan

FUTURE		CONDITIONAL	
yo	sabré	yo	sabría
tú	sabrás	tú	sabrías
él	sabrá	él	sabría
nosotros	sabremos	nosotros	sabríamos
vosotros	sabréis	vosotros	sabríais
ellos	sabrán	ellos	sabrían

IMPERFECT		PRETERITE	
yo	sabía	yo	supe
tú	sabías	tú	supiste
él	sabía	él	supo
nosotros	sabíamos	nosotros	supimos
vosotros	sabíais	vosotros	supisteis
ellos	sabían	ellos	supieron

sacar *to take out*

PAST PARTICIPLE
 sacado

GERUND
 sacando

IMPERATIVE
 saca
 sacad

PRESENT
yo	saco
tú	sacas
él	saca
nosotros	sacamos
vosotros	sacáis
ellos	sacan

FUTURE
yo	sacaré
tú	sacarás
él	sacará
nosotros	sacaremos
vosotros	sacaréis
ellos	sacarán

IMPERFECT
yo	sacaba
tú	sacabas
él	sacaba
nosotros	sacábamos
vosotros	sacabais
ellos	sacaban

PRESENT SUBJUNCTIVE
yo	saque
tú	saques
él	saque
nosotros	saquemos
vosotros	saquéis
ellos	saquen

CONDITIONAL
yo	sacaría
tú	sacarías
él	sacaría
nosotros	sacaríamos
vosotros	sacaríais
ellos	sacarían

PRETERITE
yo	saqué
tú	sacaste
él	sacó
nosotros	sacamos
vosotros	sacasteis
ellos	sacaron

salir *to go out*

PAST PARTICIPLE	IMPERATIVE
salido	**sal**
	salid

GERUND
saliendo

PRESENT		PRESENT SUBJUNCTIVE	
yo	**salgo**	yo	**salga**
tú	**sales**	tú	**salgas**
él	**sale**	él	**salga**
nosotros	**salimos**	nosotros	**salgamos**
vosotros	**salís**	vosotros	**salgáis**
ellos	**salen**	ellos	**salgan**

FUTURE		CONDITIONAL	
yo	**saldré**	yo	**saldría**
tú	**saldrás**	tú	**saldrías**
él	**saldrá**	él	**saldría**
nosotros	**saldremos**	nosotros	**saldríamos**
vosotros	**saldréis**	vosotros	**saldríais**
ellos	**saldrán**	ellos	**saldrían**

IMPERFECT		PRETERITE	
yo	**salía**	yo	**salí**
tú	**salías**	tú	**saliste**
él	**salía**	él	**salió**
nosotros	**salíamos**	nosotros	**salimos**
vosotros	**salíais**	vosotros	**salisteis**
ellos	**salían**	ellos	**salieron**

satisfacer *to satisfy*

PAST PARTICIPLE
satisfecho

IMPERATIVE
satisfaz/satisface
satisfaced

GERUND
satisfaciendo

PRESENT
yo	**satisfago**
tú	**satisfaces**
él	satisface
nosotros	satisfacemos
vosotros	satisfacéis
ellos	satisfacen

PRESENT SUBJUNCTIVE
yo	**satisfaga**
tú	**satisfagas**
él	**satisfaga**
nosotros	**satisfagamos**
vosotros	**satisfagáis**
ellos	**satisfagan**

FUTURE
yo	**satisfaré**
tú	**satisfarás**
él	**satisfará**
nosotros	**satisfaremos**
vosotros	**satisfaréis**
ellos	**satisfarán**

CONDITIONAL
yo	**satisfaría**
tú	**satisfarías**
él	**satisfaría**
nosotros	**satisfaríamos**
vosotros	**satisfaríais**
ellos	**satisfarían**

IMPERFECT
yo	satisfacía
tú	satisfacías
él	satisfacía
nosotros	satisfacíamos
vosotros	satisfacíais
ellos	satisfacían

PRETERITE
yo	**satisfice**
tú	**satisficiste**
él	**satisfizo**
nosotros	**satisficimos**
vosotros	**satisficisteis**
ellos	**satisficieron**

seguir *to follow*

PAST PARTICIPLE	IMPERATIVE
seguido	**sigue**
	seguid

GERUND
siguiendo

PRESENT

yo	sigo
tú	sigues
él	sigue
nosotros	seguimos
vosotros	seguís
ellos	**siguen**

PRESENT SUBJUNCTIVE

yo	siga
tú	sigas
él	siga
nosotros	**sigamos**
vosotros	**sigáis**
ellos	**sigan**

FUTURE

yo	seguiré
tú	seguirás
él	seguirá
nosotros	seguiremos
vosotros	seguiréis
ellos	seguirán

CONDITIONAL

yo	seguiría
tú	seguirías
él	seguiría
nosotros	seguiríamos
vosotros	seguiríais
ellos	seguirían

IMPERFECT

yo	seguía
tú	seguías
él	seguía
nosotros	seguíamos
vosotros	seguíais
ellos	seguían

PRETERITE

yo	seguí
tú	seguiste
él	siguió
nosotros	seguimos
vosotros	seguisteis
ellos	**siguieron**

sentir *to feel*

PAST PARTICIPLE
sentido

IMPERATIVE
siente
sentid

GERUND
sintiendo

PRESENT		PRESENT SUBJUNCTIVE	
yo	**siento**	yo	**sienta**
tú	**sientes**	tú	**sientas**
él	**siente**	él	**sienta**
nosotros	sentimos	**nosotros**	**sintamos**
vosotros	sentís	**vosotros**	**sintáis**
ellos	**sienten**	ellos	**sientan**

FUTURE		CONDITIONAL	
yo	sentiré	yo	sentiría
tú	sentirás	tú	sentirías
él	sentirá	él	sentiría
nosotros	sentiremos	nosotros	sentiríamos
vosotros	sentiréis	vosotros	sentiríais
ellos	sentirán	ellos	sentirían

IMPERFECT		PRETERITE	
yo	sentía	yo	sentí
tú	sentías	tú	sentiste
él	sentía	**él**	**sintió**
nosotros	sentíamos	nosotros	sentimos
vosotros	sentíais	vosotros	sentisteis
ellos	sentían	**ellos**	**sintieron**

ser *to be*

PAST PARTICIPLE
sido

GERUND
siendo

IMPERATIVE
sé
sed

PRESENT
yo	**soy**
tú	**eres**
él	**es**
nosotros	**somos**
vosotros	**sois**
ellos	**son**

FUTURE
yo	**seré**
tú	**serás**
él	**será**
nosotros	**seremos**
vosotros	**seréis**
ellos	**serán**

IMPERFECT
yo	**era**
tú	**eras**
él	**era**
nosotros	**éramos**
vosotros	**erais**
ellos	**eran**

PRESENT SUBJUNCTIVE
yo	**sea**
tú	**seas**
él	**sea**
nosotros	**seamos**
vosotros	**seáis**
ellos	**sean**

CONDITIONAL
yo	**sería**
tú	**serías**
él	**sería**
nosotros	**seríamos**
vosotros	**seríais**
ellos	**serían**

PRETERITE
yo	**fui**
tú	**fuiste**
él	**fue**
nosotros	**fuimos**
vosotros	**fuisteis**
ellos	**fueron**

tener *to have*

PAST PARTICIPLE	IMPERATIVE
tenido	ten
	tened
GERUND	
teniendo	

PRESENT	PRESENT SUBJUNCTIVE
yo tengo	yo tenga
tú tienes	tú tengas
él tiene	él tenga
nosotros tenemos	nosotros tengamos
vosotros tenéis	vosotros tengáis
ellos tienen	ellos tengan

FUTURE	CONDITIONAL
yo tendré	yo tendría
tú tendrás	tú tendrías
él tendrá	él tendría
nosotros tendremos	nosotros tendríamos
vosotros tendréis	vosotros tendríais
ellos tendrán	ellos tendrían

IMPERFECT	PRETERITE
yo tenía	yo tuve
tú tenías	tú tuviste
él tenía	él tuvo
nosotros teníamos	nosotros tuvimos
vosotros teníais	vosotros tuvisteis
ellos tenían	ellos tuvieron

torcer *to twist*

PAST PARTICIPLE
  torcido

IMPERATIVE
  tuerce
  torced

GERUND
  torciendo

PRESENT		PRESENT SUBJUNCTIVE	
yo	**tuerzo**	yo	**tuerza**
tú	**tuerces**	tú	**tuerzas**
él	**tuerce**	él	**tuerza**
nosotros	torcemos	**nosotros**	**torzamos**
vosotros	torcéis	**vosotros**	**torzáis**
ellos	**tuercen**	**ellos**	**tuerzan**

FUTURE		CONDITIONAL	
yo	torceré	yo	torcería
tú	torcerás	tú	torcerías
él	torcerá	él	torcería
nosotros	torceremos	nosotros	torceríamos
vosotros	torceréis	vosotros	torceríais
ellos	torcerán	ellos	torcerían

IMPERFECT		PRETERITE	
yo	torcía	yo	torcí
tú	torcías	tú	torciste
él	torcía	él	torció
nosotros	torcíamos	nosotros	torcimos
vosotros	torcíais	vosotros	torcisteis
ellos	torcían	ellos	torcieron

traer *to bring*

PAST PARTICIPLE
traído

IMPERATIVE
trae
traed

GERUND
trayendo

PRESENT

yo	**traigo**
tú	traes
él	trae
nosotros	traemos
vosotros	traéis
ellos	traen

PRESENT SUBJUNCTIVE

yo	**traiga**
tú	**traigas**
él	**traiga**
nosotros	**traigamos**
vosotros	**traigáis**
ellos	**traigan**

FUTURE

yo	traeré
tú	traerás
él	traerá
nosotros	traeremos
vosotros	traeréis
ellos	traerán

CONDITIONAL

yo	traería
tú	traerías
él	traería
nosotros	traeríamos
vosotros	traeríais
ellos	traerían

IMPERFECT

yo	traía
tú	traías
él	traía
nosotros	traíamos
vosotros	traíais
ellos	traían

PRETERITE

yo	**traje**
tú	**trajiste**
él	**trajo**
nosotros	**trajimos**
vosotros	**trajisteis**
ellos	**trajeron**

valer *to be worth*

PAST PARTICIPLE
valido

IMPERATIVE
vale
valed

GERUND
valiendo

PRESENT
       yo **valgo**
       tú **vales**
       él **vale**
  nosotros **valemos**
  vosotros **valéis**
     ellos **valen**

PRESENT SUBJUNCTIVE
       yo **valga**
       tú **valgas**
       él **valga**
  nosotros **valgamos**
  vosotros **valgáis**
     ellos **valgan**

FUTURE
       yo **valdré**
       tú **valdrás**
       él **valdrá**
  nosotros **valdremos**
  vosotros **valdréis**
     ellos **valdrán**

CONDITIONAL
       yo **valdría**
       tú **valdrías**
       él **valdría**
  nosotros **valdríamos**
  vosotros **valdríais**
     ellos **valdrían**

IMPERFECT
       yo **valía**
       tú **valías**
       él **valía**
  nosotros **valíamos**
  vosotros **valíais**
     ellos **valían**

PRETERITE
       yo **valí**
       tú **valiste**
       él **valió**
  nosotros **valimos**
  vosotros **valisteis**
     ellos **valieron**

vencer to win

PAST PARTICIPLE
vencido

IMPERATIVE
vence
venced

GERUND
venciendo

PRESENT
yo **venzo**
tú vences
él vence
nosotros vencemos
vosotros vencéis
ellos vencen

PRESENT SUBJUNCTIVE
yo **venza**
tú **venzas**
él **venza**
nosotros **venzamos**
vosotros **venzáis**
ellos **venzan**

FUTURE
yo venceré
tú vencerás
él vencerá
nosotros venceremos
vosotros venceréis
ellos vencerán

CONDITIONAL
yo vencería
tú vencerías
él vencería
nosotros venceríamos
vosotros venceríais
ellos vencerían

IMPERFECT
yo vencía
tú vencías
él vencía
nosotros vencíamos
vosotros vencíais
ellos vencían

PRETERITE
yo vencí
tú venciste
él venció
nosotros vencimos
vosotros vencisteis
ellos vencieron

venir *to come*

PAST PARTICIPLE
venido

IMPERATIVE
ven
venid

GERUND
viniendo

PRESENT

yo	vengo
tú	vienes
él	viene
nosotros	venimos
vosotros	venís
ellos	vienen

PRESENT SUBJUNCTIVE

yo	venga
tú	vengas
él	venga
nosotros	vengamos
vosotros	vengáis
ellos	vengan

FUTURE

yo	vendré
tú	vendrás
él	vendrá
nosotros	vendremos
vosotros	vendréis
ellos	vendrán

CONDITIONAL

yo	vendría
tú	vendrías
él	vendría
nosotros	vendríamos
vosotros	vendríais
ellos	vendrían

IMPERFECT

yo	venía
tú	venías
él	venía
nosotros	veníamos
vosotros	veníais
ellos	venían

PRETERITE

yo	vine
tú	viniste
él	vino
nosotros	vinimos
vosotros	vinisteis
ellos	vinieron

ver *to see*

PAST PARTICIPLE
visto

IMPERATIVE
ve
ved

GERUND
viendo

PRESENT		PRESENT SUBJUNCTIVE	
yo	veo	yo	vea
tú	ves	tú	veas
él	ve	él	vea
nosotros	vemos	nosotros	veamos
vosotros	veis	vosotros	veáis
ellos	ven	ellos	vean

FUTURE		CONDITIONAL	
yo	veré	yo	vería
tú	verás	tú	verías
él	verá	él	vería
nosotros	veremos	nosotros	veríamos
vosotros	veréis	vosotros	veríais
ellos	verán	ellos	verían

IMPERFECT		PRETERITE	
yo	veía	yo	vi
tú	veías	tú	viste
él	veía	él	vio
nosotros	veíamos	nosotros	vimos
vosotros	veíais	vosotros	visteis
ellos	veían	ellos	vieron

volcar *to overturn*

PAST PARTICIPLE
volcado

GERUND
volcando

IMPERATIVE
vuelca
volcad

PRESENT
yo	**vuelco**
tú	**vuelcas**
él	**vuelca**
nosotros	volcamos
vosotros	volcáis
ellos	**vuelcan**

FUTURE
yo	volcaré
tú	volcarás
él	volcará
nosotros	volcaremos
vosotros	volcaréis
ellos	volcarán

IMPERFECT
yo	volcaba
tú	volcabas
él	volcaba
nosotros	volcábamos
vosotros	volcabais
ellos	volcaban

PRESENT SUBJUNCTIVE
yo	**vuelque**
tú	**vuelques**
él	**vuelque**
nosotros	**volquemos**
vosotros	**volquéis**
ellos	**vuelquen**

CONDITIONAL
yo	volcaría
tú	volcarías
él	volcaría
nosotros	volcaríamos
vosotros	volcaríais
ellos	volcarían

PRETERITE
yo	**volqué**
tú	volcaste
él	volcó
nosotros	volcamos
vosotros	volcasteis
ellos	volcaron

volver to return

PAST PARTICIPLE
vuelto

IMPERATIVE
vuelve
volved

GERUND
volviendo

PRESENT

yo	**vuelvo**
tú	**vuelves**
él	**vuelve**
nosotros	volvemos
vosotros	volvéis
ellos	**vuelven**

PRESENT SUBJUNCTIVE

yo	**vuelva**
tú	**vuelvas**
él	**vuelva**
nosotros	volvamos
vosotros	volváis
ellos	**vuelvan**

FUTURE

yo	volveré
tú	volverás
él	volverá
nosotros	volveremos
vosotros	volveréis
ellos	volverán

CONDITIONAL

yo	volvería
tú	volverías
él	volvería
nosotros	volveríamos
vosotros	volveríais
ellos	volverían

IMPERFECT

yo	volvía
tú	volvías
él	volvía
nosotros	volvíamos
vosotros	volvíais
ellos	volvían

PRETERITE

yo	volví
tú	volviste
él	volvió
nosotros	volvimos
vosotros	volvisteis
ellos	volvieron

zurcir to darn

PAST PARTICIPLE
zurcido

IMPERATIVE
zurce
zurcid

GERUND
zurciendo

PRESENT		PRESENT SUBJUNCTIVE	
yo	zurzo	yo	zurza
tú	zurces	tú	zurzas
él	zurce	él	zurza
nosotros	zurcimos	nosotros	zurzamos
vosotros	zurcís	vosotros	zurzáis
ellos	zurcen	ellos	zurzan

FUTURE		CONDITIONAL	
yo	zurciré	yo	zurciría
tú	zurcirás	tú	zurcirías
él	zurcirá	él	zurciría
nosotros	zurciremos	nosotros	zurciríamos
vosotros	zurciréis	vosotros	zurciríais
ellos	zurcirán	ellos	zurcirían

IMPERFECT		PRETERITE	
yo	zurcía	yo	zurcí
tú	zurcías	tú	zurciste
él	zurcía	él	zurció
nosotros	zurcíamos	nosotros	zurcimos
vosotros	zurcíais	vosotros	zurcisteis
ellos	zurcían	ellos	zurcieron

The following pages, 163 to 186, contain an index of over 2,800 commonly used verbs cross-referred to the appropriate conjugation model.

- Regular verbs belonging to the first, second and third conjugation are numbered 1, 2 and 3 respectively. For the regular conjugations see pp. 6 to 13.

- Irregular verbs are numerically cross-referred to the appropriate model as conjugated on pp. 82 to 161. Thus, **alzar** is cross-referred to p. 100 where **cruzar**, the model for this verb group, is conjugated.

- Verbs which are most commonly used in the reflexive form — e.g. **amodorrarse** — have been cross-referred to the appropriate non-reflexive model. For the full conjugation of a reflexive verb, see pp. 28 to 31.

- Verbs printed in bold — e.g. **abrir** — are themselves models.

- Superior numbers refer you to notes on p. 187 which indicate how the verb differs from its model.

barajar	1	bostezar	100	caminar	1
barbotar	1	botar	1	campar	1
barnizar	100	bracear	1	camuflar	1
barrenar	1	bramar	1	canalizar	100
barrer	2	bricolajear	1	cancelar	1
barruntar	1	brillar	1	canjear	1
basar	1	brincar	146	canonizar	100
bascular	1	brindar	1	cansar	1
bastar	1	bromear	1	cantar	1
batallar	1	broncearse	1	canturrear	1
batir	3	brotar	1	capacitar	1
bautizar	100	bruñir	116	capar	1
beber	2	bucear	1	capitalizar	100
bendecir	91	bufar	1	capitanear	1
beneficiar	1	bullir	116	capitular	1
berrear	1	burbujear	1	captar	1
besar	1	burlar	1	capturar	1
besuquear	1	buscar	146	caracolear	1
bifurcarse	146	cabalgar	131	caracterizar	100
birlar	1	cabecear	1	carbonizar	100
biselar	1	**caber**	92	carcomer	2
bizquear	1	cacarear	1	carear	1
blandir	3	cachear	1	carecer	99
blanquear	1	caducar	146	cargar	131
blasfemar	1	**caer**	93	casar	1
blasonar	1	calar	1	cascar	146
blindar	1	calcar	146	castigar	131
bloquear	1	calcinar	1	castrar	1
bobinar	1	calcular	1	catar	1
bocetar	1	caldear	1	caucionar	1
bogar	131	calentar	133	causar	1
boicotear	1	calibrar	1	cautivar	1
bombardear	1	calificar	146	cavar	1
bombear	1	calmar	1	cavilar	1
boquear	1	calumniar	1	cazar	100
borbotear	1	calzar	100	cebar	1
bordar	1	callar	1	cecear	1
bordear	1	callejear	1	ceder	2
borrar	1	cambiar	1	cegar	128
bosquejar	1	camelar	1	cejar	1

conectar	1	contagiar	1	cortejar	1
confeccionar	1	contaminar	1	cosechar	1
conferir	150	**contar**	98	coser	2
confesar	133	contemplar	1	costar	98
configurar	1	contemporizar	100	cotejar	1
confiar	110	contender	109	cotizar	100
confinar	1	contener	152	crear	1
confirmar	1	contentar	1	**crecer**	99
confiscar	146	contestar	1	creer	122
conformar	1	continuar	84	criar	110
confortar	1	contradecir	103	cribar	1
confrontar	1	contraer	154	crispar	1
confundir	3	contrapesar	1	cristalizar	100
congelar	1	contrariar	110	criticar	146
congeniar	1	contrarrestar	1	crucificar	146
congratular	1	contrastar	1	crujir	3
conjeturar	1	contratar	1	**cruzar**	100
conjugar	131	contravenir	157	cuadrar	1
conllevar	1	contribuir	97	cuajar	1
conmemorar	1	convalecer	99	cuantificar	146
conminar	1	convencer	99	cuartear	1
conmover	126	convenir	157	cubrir	101
conocer	99	converger	95	cuchichear	1
conquistar	1	convergir	104	cuidar	1
consagrar	1	conversar	1	culebrear	1
conseguir	149	convertir	150	culpar	1
consentir	150	convidar	1	cultivar	1
conservar	1	convocar	146	cumplimentar	1
considerar	1	cooperar	1	cumplir	3
consistir	3	coordinar	1	curar	1
consolar	98	copiar	1	curiosear	1
consolidar	1	coquetear	1	custodiar	1
conspirar	1	coronar	1	chamuscar	146
constar	1	corregir	107	chantajear	1
constituir	97	correr	2	chapotear	1
constreñir	140	corresponder	2	chapurrear	1
construir	97	corroborar	1	chapuzarse	100
consultar	1	corroer	93	charlar	1
consumar	1	corromper	2	chasquear	1
consumir	3	cortar	1	chequear	1

Notes

The notes below indicate special peculiarities of individual verbs. When only some forms of a given tense are affected, all these are shown. When all forms of the tense are affected, only the 1st and 2nd persons are shown, followed by *etc*.

1 Gerund 2 Past Participle 3 Present 4 Preterite 5 Present Subjunctive 6 Imperfect Subjunctive

1) **acaecer, acontecer, amanecer, anochecer, competer, deshelar, escampar, granizar, helar, nevar, nublarse, relampaguear, tronar, verdear, verdecer**: used almost exclusively in infinitive and 3rd person singular

2) **asir** 3 asgo 5 asga, asgas *etc*

3) **atañer** 1 atañendo 4 atañó: see also 1) above

4) **balbucir** 3 balbuceo 5 balbucee, balbucees *etc*

5) **concernir** 3 concierne, conciernen 5 concierna, conciernan: only used in 3rd person

6) **degollar** 3 degüello, degüellas, degüella, degüellan 5 degüelle, degüelles, degüellen

7) **delinquir** 3 delinco 5 delinca, delincas *etc*

8) **desasir** 3 desasgo 5 desasga, desasgas *etc*

9) **discernir** 3 discierno, disciernes, discierne, disciernen 5 discierna, disciernas, disciernan

10) **enraizar** 3 enraízo, enraízas, enraíza, enraízan 5 enraíce, enraíces, enraícen

11) **pudrir** 2 podrido

12) **rehuir** 3 rehúyo, rehúyes, rehúye, rehúyen 5 rehúya, rehúyas, rehúyan

13) **roer** 4 royó, royeron 6 royera, royeras *etc*

14) **soler**: used only in present and imperfect indicative

15) **yacer** 3 yazgo, or yazco, or yago 5 yazga *etc*, or yazca *etc*, or yaga *etc*

The Gender of Nouns

In Spanish, all nouns are either masculine or feminine, whether denoting people, animals or things. Unlike English, there is no neuter gender for inanimate objects and abstract nouns. Gender is largely unpredictable and has to be learnt for each noun. However, the following guidelines will help you determine the gender for certain types of nouns.

● Nouns denoting male people and animals are usually — but not always — masculine, e.g.

un hombre	**un toro**
a man	a bull
un enfermero	**un semental**
a (male) nurse	a stallion

● Nouns denoting female people and animals are usually — but not always — feminine, e.g.

una niña	**una vaca**
a girl	a cow
una enfermera	**una yegua**
a nurse	a mare

● Some nouns are masculine OR feminine depending on the sex of the person to whom they refer, e.g.

un camarada	**una camarada**
a (male) comrade	a (female) comrade
un belga	**una belga**
a Belgian (man)	a Belgian (woman)
un marroquí	**una marroquí**
a Moroccan (man)	a Moroccan (woman)

● Other nouns referring to either men or women have only one gender which applies to both, e.g.

una persona	**una visita**
a person	a visitor
una víctima	**una estrella**
a victim	a star

● Often the ending of a noun indicates its gender. Shown below are some of the most important to guide you.

Masculine endings

-o
un clavo *a nail,* un plátano *a banana*
EXCEPTIONS: **mano** *hand,* **foto** *photograph,* **moto(cicleta)** *motorbike*

-l
un tonel *a barrel,* un hotel *a hotel*
EXCEPTIONS: **cal** *lime,* **cárcel** *prison,* **catedral** *cathedral,* **col** *cabbage,* **miel** *honey,* **piel** *skin,* **sal** *salt,* **señal** *sign*

-r
un tractor *a tractor,* el altar *the altar*
EXCEPTIONS: **coliflor** *cauliflower,* **flor** *flower,* **labor** *task*

-y
el rey *the king,* un buey *an ox*
EXCEPTION: **ley** *law*

Feminine endings

-a
una casa *a house,* la cara *the face*
EXCEPTIONS: **día** *day,* **mapa** *map,* **planeta** *planet,* **tranvía** *tram,* and most words ending in -ma (tema *subject,* problema *problem,* etc)

-ión
una canción *a song,* una procesión *a procession;* EXCEPTIONS: most nouns not ending in -ción or -sión, e.g. **avión** *aeroplane,* **camión** *lorry,* **gorrión** *sparrow*

-dad, -tad,
-tud
una ciudad *a town,* la libertad *freedom,* una multitud *a crowd*

-ed
una pared *a wall,* la sed *thirst*
EXCEPTION: **césped** *lawn*

-itis
una faringitis *pharyngitis,* la celulitis *cellulitis*

-iz
una perdiz *a partridge,* una matriz *a matrix*
EXCEPTIONS: **lápiz** *pencil,* **maíz** *corn,* **tapiz** *a tapestry*

-sis
una tesis *a thesis,* una dosis *a dose*
EXCEPTIONS: **análisis** *analysis,* **énfasis** *emphasis,* **paréntesis** *parenthesis*

-umbre
la podredumbre *rot,* la muchedumbre *crowd*

Gender of nouns (ctd.)

Some nouns change meaning according to gender. The most common are set out below:

	MASCULINE	FEMININE	
capital	capital (money)	capital (city)	(→1)
clave	harpsichord	clue	
cólera	cholera	anger	(→2)
cometa	comet	kite	
corriente	current month	current	
corte	cut	court (royal)	(→3)
coma	coma	comma	(→4)
cura	priest	cure	(→5)
físico/a	physique	physics	
frente	front (in war)	forehead	(→6)
guardia	guard(sman)	guard	(→7)
guía	guide (person)	guide(book)	(→8)
moral	mulberry tree	morals	
orden	order (arrangement)	order (command)	(→9)
ordenanza	office boy	ordinance	
papa	Pope	potato	
parte	dispatch	part	(→10)
pendiente	earring	slope	
pez	fish	pitch	
policía	policeman	police	
radio	radius, radium	radio	

1 **Invirtieron mucho capital**
  They invested a lot of capital
  La capital es muy fea
  The capital city is very ugly

2 **Es difícil luchar contra el cólera**   **Montó en cólera**
  Cholera is difficult to combat   He got angry

3 **Me encanta tu corte de pelo**
  I love your haircut
  Se trasladó la corte a Madrid
  The court was moved to Madrid

4 **Entró en un coma profundo**
  He went into a deep coma
  Aquí hace falta una coma
  You need to put a comma here

5 **¿Quién es? — El cura**   **No tiene cura**
  Who is it? — The priest   It's hopeless

6 **Han mandado a su hijo al frente**
  Her son has been sent to the front
  Tiene la frente muy ancha
  She has a very broad forehead

7 **Vino un guardia de tráfico**
  A traffic policeman came
  Están relevando la guardia ahora
  They're changing the guard now

8 **Nuestro guía nos hizo reír a carcajadas**
  Our guide had us falling about laughing
  Busco una guía turística
  I'm looking for a guidebook

9 **Están en orden alfabético**
  They're in alphabetical order
  No hemos recibido la orden de pago
  We haven't had the payment order

10 **Le mandó un parte al general**
  He sent a dispatch to the general
  En alguna parte debe estar
  It must be somewhere or other

Gender: the formation of feminines

As in English, male and female are sometimes differentiated by
the use of two quite separate words, e.g.

mi marido	**mi mujer**
my husband	*my wife*
un toro	**una vaca**
a bull	*a cow*

There are, however, some words in Spanish which show this
distinction by the form of their ending

- Nouns ending in **-o** change to **-a** to form the feminine (→1)

- If the masculine singular form already ends in **-a**, no further **-a**
  is added to the feminine (→2)

- If the last letter of the masculine singular form is a consonant,
  an **-a** is normally added in the feminine* (→3)

Feminine forms to note

MASCULINE	FEMININE	
el abad	**la abadesa**	*abbott/abbess*
un actor	**una actriz**	*actor/actress*
el alcalde	**la alcaldesa**	*mayor/mayoress*
el conde	**la condesa**	*count/countess*
el duque	**la duquesa**	*duke/duchess*
el emperador	**la emperatriz**	*emperor/empress*
un poeta	**una poetisa**	*a poet*
el príncipe	**la princesa**	*prince/princess*
el rey	**la reina**	*king/queen*
un sacerdote	**una sacerdotisa**	*priest/priestess*
un tigre	**una tigresa**	*tiger/tigress*
el zar	**la zarina**	*czar/czarina*

*If the last syllable has an accent, it disappears in the feminine
(see p. 292) (→4)

1 un **amigo**
a (male) friend
un **empleado**
a (male) employee
un **gato**
a cat

una **amiga**
a (female) friend
una **empleada**
a (female) employee
una **gata**
a (female) cat

2 un **deportista**
a sportsman
un **colega**
a (male) colleague
un **camarada**
a (male) comrade

una **deportista**
a sportswoman
una **colega**
a (female) colleague
una **camarada**
a (female) comrade

3 un **español**
a Spaniard, a Spanish man
un **vendedor**
a salesman
un **jugador**
a player (man)

una **española**
a Spanish woman
una **vendedora**
a saleswoman
una **jugadora**
a player (woman)

4 un **lapón**
a Laplander (man)
un **león**
a lion
un **neocelandés**
a New Zealander (man)

una **lapona**
a Laplander (woman)
una **leona**
a lioness
una **neocelandesa**
a New Zealander (woman)

The formation of plurals

- Nouns ending in an unstressed vowel add **-s** to the singular form (→1)

- Nouns ending in a consonant or a stressed vowel add **-es** to the singular form (→2)

  Exceptions:

café	coffee shop	(plur: **cafés**)
mamá	mummy	(plur: **mamás**)
papá	daddy	(plur: **papás**)
pie	foot	(plur: **pies**)
sofá	sofa	(plur: **sofás**)
té	tea	(plur: **tes**)

  and words of foreign origin ending in a consonant, eg:

coñac	brandy	(plur: **coñacs**)
jersey	jumper	(plur: **jerseys**)

  It should be noted that:
  - nouns ending in **-n** or **-s** with an accent on the last syllable drop this accent in the plural (see p. 292) (→3)
  - nouns ending in **-n** with the stress on the second-last syllable in the singular add an accent to that syllable in the plural in order to show the correct position for stress (see p. 292) (→4)
  - nouns ending in **-z** change this to **c** in the plural in order to maintain the same sound (→5)

- Nouns with an unstressed final syllable ending in **-s** do not change in the plural (→6)

1 la casa   las casas
   the house   the houses
   el auto   los autos
   the car   the cars

2 un rumor   unos rumores
   a rumour   (some) rumours
   un jabalí   unos jabalíes
   a boar   (some) boars

3 la canción   las canciones
   the song   the songs
   el autobús   los autobuses
   the bus   the buses

4 un examen   unos exámenes
   an exam   (some) exams
   un crimen   unos crímenes
   a crime   (some) crimes

5 la luz   las luces
   the light   the lights

6 un paraguas   unos paraguas
   an umbrella   (some) umbrellas
   la dosis   las dosis
   the dose   the doses
   el lunes   los lunes
   Monday   Mondays

The Definite Article

	WITH MASC. NOUN	WITH FEM. NOUN	
SING.	**el**	**la**	*the*
PLUR.	**los**	**las**	*the*

- The gender and number of the noun determines the form of the article (→1)
  It should be noted, however, that if the article comes directly before a feminine singular noun which starts with a stressed **a-** or **ha-**, the masculine form **el** is used instead of the feminine **la** (→2)

- For uses of the definite article see p. 199

- **a + el** becomes **al** (→3)

- **de + el** becomes **del** (→4)

Continued

1 el tren
the train
el actor
the actor
los hoteles
the hotels
los profesores
the teachers

la estación
the station
la actriz
the actress
las escuelas
the schools
las mujeres
the women

2 el agua
the water
el hacha
the axe

BUT

BUT

la misma agua
the same water
la mejor hacha
the best axe

3 al cine
to the cinema
al empleado
to the employee
al hospital
to the hospital

4 del departamento
from/of the department
del autor
from/of the author
del presidente
from/of the president

Uses of the definite article

While the definite article is used in much the same way in Spanish as it is in English, its use is more widespread in Spanish. Unlike English the definite article is also used:

- with abstract nouns, except when following certain prepositions (→**1**)

- in generalizations, especially with plural or uncountable* nouns (→**2**)

- with parts of the body (→**3**)
  'Ownership' is often indicated by an indirect object pronoun or a reflexive pronoun (→**4**)

- with titles/ranks/professions followed by a proper name (→**5**)
  Exceptions: with **Don/Doña, San/Santo(a)** (→**6**)

- before nouns of official, academic and religious buildings, and names of meals and games (→**7**)

- The definite article is NOT used with nouns in apposition unless those nouns are individualized (→**8**)

* An uncountable noun is one which cannot be used in the plural or with an indefinite article, e.g. **el acero** steel, **la leche** milk.

1 **Los precios suben**
Prices are rising
El tiempo es oro
Time is money
BUT
con pasión   **sin esperanza**
with passion   without hope

2 **No me gusta el café**
I don't like coffee
Los niños necesitan ser queridos
Children need to be loved

3 **Vuelva la cabeza hacia la izquierda**
Turn your head to the left
No puedo mover las piernas
I can't move my legs

4 **La cabeza me da vueltas**
My head is spinning
Lávate las manos
Wash your hands

5 **El rey Jorge III**   **el capitan Menéndez**
King George III   Captain Menéndez
el doctor Ochoa   **el señor Ramírez**
Doctor Ochoa   Mr. Ramírez

6 **Don Arturo Ruiz**   **Santa Teresa**
Mr. Arturo Ruiz   Saint Teresa

7 **en la cárcel**   **en la universidad**   **en la iglesia**
in prison   at university   at church
la cena   **el tenis**   **el ajedrez**
dinner   tennis   chess

8 **Madrid, capital de España, es la ciudad que ...**
Madrid, the capital of Spain, is the city which ...
BUT
Maria Callas, la famosa cantante de ópera ...
Maria Callas, the famous opera singer ...

The Indefinite Article

	WITH MASC. NOUN	WITH FEM. NOUN	
SING.	**un**	**una**	a
PLUR.	**unos**	**unas**	some

The indefinite article is used in Spanish largely as it is in English
EXCEPT:

- There is no article when a person's profession is being stated
  (→1)
  The article is used, however, when the profession is qualified
  by an adjective (→2)

- The article is not used with the following words:

otro	another	(→3)
cierto	certain	(→4)
semejante	such (a)	(→5)
tal	such (a)	(→6)
cien	a hundred	(→7)
mil	a thousand	(→8)
sin	without	(→9)
qué	what a	(→10)

- There is no article with a noun in apposition (→11). When an
  abstract noun is qualified by an adjective, the indefinite article
  is used, but is not translated in English (→12)

1   **Es profesor**   **Mi madre es enfermera**
    He's a teacher   My mother is a nurse
2   **Es un buen médico**
    He's a good doctor
    Se hizo una escritora célebre
    She became a famous writer
3   **otro libro**
    another book
4   **cierta calle**
    a certain street
5   **semejante ruido**
    such a noise
6   **tal mentira**
    such a lie
7   **cien soldados**
    a hundred soldiers
8   **mil años**
    a thousand years
9   **sin casa**
    without a house
10 **¡qué sorpresa!**
    what a surprise!
11 **Baroja, gran escritor de la Generación del 98**
    Baroja, a great writer of the 'Generación del 98'
12 **con una gran sabiduría/un valor admirable**
    with great wisdom/admirable courage
    Dieron pruebas de una sangre fría increíble
    They showed incredible coolness
    una película de un mal gusto espantoso
    a film in appallingly bad taste

The Article 'lo'

This is never used with a noun. Instead, it is used in the following ways:

- As an intensifier before an adjective or adverb in the construction

  lo + adjective/adverb + **que** (→1)

  Note that the adjective agrees with the noun it refers to (→2)

- With an adjective or participle to form an abstract noun (→3)

- In the phrase **lo de** to refer to a subject of which speaker and listener are already aware. It can often be translated as *the business/affair of/about . . .* (→4)

- In set expressions, the commonest of which are:

a lo mejor	*maybe, perhaps*	(→5)
a lo lejos	*in the distance*	(→6)
a lo largo de	*along, through*	(→7)
por lo menos	*at least*	(→8)
por lo tanto	*therefore, so*	(→9)
por lo visto	*apparently*	(→10)

1   **No sabíamos lo pequeña que era la casa**
     We didn't know how small the house was
     Sé lo mucho que te gusta la música
     I know how much you like music

2   **No te imaginas lo simpáticos que son**
     You can't imagine how nice they are
     Ya sabes lo buenas que son estas manzanas
     You already know how good these apples are

3   **Lo bueno de eso es que ...**
     The good thing about it is that ...
     Sentimos mucho lo ocurrido
     We are very sorry about what happened

4   **Lo de ayer es mejor que lo olvides**
     It's better if you forget what happened yesterday
     Lo de tu hermano me preocupa mucho
     The business about your brother worries me very much

5   **A lo mejor ha salido**
     Perhaps he's gone out

6   **A lo lejos se veían unas casas**
     Some houses could be seen in the distance

7   **A lo largo de su vida**
     Throughout his life
     A lo largo de la carretera
     Along the road

8   **Hubo por lo menos cincuenta heridos**
     At least fifty people were injured

9   **No hemos recibido ninguna instrucción al respecto, y por lo tanto no podemos ...**
     We have not received any instructions about it, therefore we cannot ...

10   **Por lo visto, no viene**
     Apparently he's not coming OR He's not coming, it seems

Adjectives

Most adjectives agree in number and in gender with the noun or pronoun.
Note that:
— if the adjective refers to two or more singular nouns of the same gender, a plural ending of that gender is required (→**1**)
— if the adjective refers to two or more singular nouns of different genders, a masculine plural ending is required (→**2**)

The formation of feminines

- Adjectives ending in **-o** change to **-a** (→**3**)

- Some groups of adjectives add **-a**:
  — adjectives of nationality or geographical origin (→**4**)
  — adjectives ending in **-or** (except irregular comparatives: see p. 210), **-án, -ón, -in** (→**5**)
  Note: when there is an accent on the last syllable, it disappears in the feminine (see p. 292)

- Other adjectives do not change (→**6**)

The formation of plurals

- Adjectives ending in an unstressed vowel add **-s** (→**7**)

- Adjectives ending in a stressed vowel or a consonant add **-es** (→**8**)
  Note that:
  — if there is an accent on the last syllable of a word ending in a consonant, it will disappear in the plural (see p. 292) (→**9**)
  — if the last letter is a z it will become a c in the plural (→**10**)

1   **la lengua y la literatura españolas**
    (the) Spanish language and literature

2   **Nunca había visto árboles y flores tan raros**
    I had never seen such strange trees and flowers

3   **mi hermano pequeño**   **mi hermana pequeña**
    my little brother   my little sister

4   **un chico español**   **una chica española**
    a Spanish boy   a Spanish girl
    el equipo barcelonés   **la vida barcelonesa**
    the team from Barcelona   the Barcelona way of life

5   **un niño encantador**   **una niña encantadora**
    a charming little boy   a charming little girl
    un hombre holgazán   **una mujer holgazana**
    an idle man   an idle woman
    un gesto burlón   **una sonrisa burlona**
    a mocking gesture   a mocking smile
    un chico cantarín   **una chica cantarina**
    a boy fond of singing   a girl fond of singing

6   **un final feliz**   **una infancia feliz**
    a happy ending   a happy childhood
    mi amigo belga   **mi amiga belga**
    my Belgian (male) friend   my Belgian (female) friend
    el vestido verde   **la blusa verde**
    the green dress   the green blouse

7   **el último tren**   **los últimos trenes**
    the last train   the last trains
    una casa vieja   **unas casas viejas**
    an old house   (some) old houses

8   **un médico iraní**   **unos médicos iraníes**
    an Iranian doctor   (some) Iranian doctors
    un examen fácil   **unos exámenes fáciles**
    an easy exam   (some) easy exams

9   **un río francés**   **unos ríos franceses**
    a French river   (some) French rivers

10 **un día feliz**   **unos días felices**
    a happy day   (some) happy days

Invariable Adjectives

Some adjectives and other parts of speech when used adjectivally never change in the feminine or plural.
The commonest of these are:
— nouns denoting colour (→1)
— compound adjectives (→2)
— nouns used as adjectives (→3)

Shortening of Adjectives

- The following drop the final -o before a masculine singular noun:
  bueno *good* (→4)
  malo *bad*
  alguno* *some* (→5)
  ninguno* *none*
  uno* *one* (→6)
  primero *first* (→7)
  tercero *third*
  postrero *last* (→8)
*Note that an accent is required to show the correct position for stress.

- **Grande** *big, great* is usually shortened to **gran** before a masculine OR feminine singular noun (→9)

- **Santo** *Saint* changes to **San** except with saints' names beginning with **Do-** or **To-** (→10)

- **Ciento** *a hundred* is shortened to **cien** (→11)

- **Cualquiera** drops the final -a before a masculine OR feminine singular noun (→12)

1 **los vestidos naranja**
   the orange dresses

2 **las chaquetas azul marino**
   the navy blue jackets

3 **bebés probeta**   **mujeres soldado**
   test-tube babies   women soldiers

4 **un buen libro**
   a good book

5 **algún libro**
   some book

6 **cuarenta y un años**
   forty one years

7 **el primer hijo**
   the first child

8 **un postrer deseo**
   a last wish

9 **un gran actor**   **una gran decepción**
   a great actor   a great disappointment

10 **San Antonio**   **Santo Tomás**
   Saint Anthony   Saint Thomas

11 **cien años**
   a hundred years
   cien millones
   a hundred million

12 **cualquier día**   **a cualquier hora**
   any day   any time

Comparatives and Superlatives

Comparatives

These are formed using the following constructions:

más ... (que)	*more ... (than)*	(→1)
menos ... (que)	*less ... (than)*	(→2)
tanto ... como	*as ... as*	(→3)
tan ... como	*as ... as*	(→4)
tan ... que	*so ... that*	(→5)
demasiado ...	*too ...*	
bastante ... } para	*enough ...* } *to*	(→6)
suficiente ...	*enough ...*	

● 'Than' followed by a clause is translated by **de lo que** (→7)

Superlatives

These are formed using the following constructions:

el/la/los/las más ... (que)	*the most ... (that)*	(→8)
el/la/los/las menos ... (que)	*the least ... (that)*	(→9)

● After a superlative the preposition **de** is often translated as *in* (→10)

● The absolute superlative (*very, most, extremely* + adjective) is expressed in Spanish by **muy** + adjective, or by adding **-ísimo/a/os/as** to the adjective when it ends in a consonant, or to its stem (adjective minus final vowel) when it ends in a vowel (→11)
Note that it is sometimes necessary to change the spelling of the adjective when **-ísimo** is added, in order to maintain the same sound (see p. 296) (→12)

Continued

1 una razón **más** seria
   a **more** serious reason
   Es más alto que mi hermano
   He's **taller than** my brother

2 una película **menos** conocida
   a **less** well known film
   Luis es menos tímido que tú
   Luis is less shy than you

3 Pablo tenía **tanto** miedo **como** yo
   Paul was **as** frightened **as** I was

4 No es **tan** grande **como** creía
   It isn't **as** big **as** I thought

5 El examen era **tan** difícil **que** nadie aprobó
   The exam was **so** difficult **that** nobody passed

6 No tengo **suficiente** dinero para comprarlo
   I haven't got **enough** money to buy it

7 Está **más** cansada **de lo que** parece
   She is **more** tired **than** she seems

8 el caballo **más** veloz   la casa **más** pequeña
   the **fastest** horse   the **smallest** house
   los días **más** lluviosos   las manzanas **más** maduras
   the **wettest** days   the **ripest** apples

9 el hombre **menos** simpático   la niña **menos** habladora
   the **least** likeable man   the **least** talkative girl
   los cuadros **menos** bonitos   las camisas **menos** viejas
   the **least** attractive paintings the **least** old shirts

10 la estación **más** ruidosa **de** Londres
   the **noisiest** station **in** London

11 Este libro es **muy** interesante   Tienen un coche rapid**ísimo**
   This book is **very** interesting   They have an **extremely** fast car
   Era facil**ísimo** de hacer
   It was **very** easy to make

12 Mi tío era **muy** rico   Se hizo riqu**ísimo**
   My uncle was **very** rich   He became **extremely** rich
   un león **muy** feroz   un tigre feroc**ísimo**
   a **very** ferocious lion   an **extremely** ferocious tiger

Comparatives and Superlatives (ctd.)

Adjectives with irregular comparatives/superlatives

ADJECTIVE	COMPARATIVE	SUPERLATIVE
bueno	**mejor**	**el mejor**
good	*better*	*the best*
malo	**peor**	**el peor**
bad	*worse*	*the worst*
grande	**mayor**	**el mayor**
big	OR	OR
	más grande	**el más grande**
	bigger; older	*the biggest; the oldest*
pequeño	**menor**	**el menor**
small	OR	OR
	más pequeño	**el más pequeño**
	smaller; younger; lesser	*the smallest; the youngest; the least*

- The irregular comparative and superlative forms of **grande** and **pequeño** are used mainly to express:
  - age, in which case they come after the noun (→1)
  - abstract size and degrees of importance, in which case they come before the noun (→2)

  The regular forms are used mainly to express physical size (→3)

- Irregular comparatives and superlatives have one form for both masculine and feminine, but always agree in number with the noun (→1)

1 **mis hermanos mayores**
my older brothers
la hija menor
the youngest daughter

2 **el menor ruido**
the slightest sound
las mayores dificultades
the biggest difficulties

3 **Este plato es más grande que aquél**
This plate is bigger than that one
Mi casa es más pequeña que la tuya
My house is smaller than yours

Demonstrative Adjectives

	MASCULINE	FEMININE	
SING.	este	esta	*this*
	ese	esa	*that*
	aquel	aquella	
PLUR.	estos	estas	*these*
	esos	esas	*those*
	aquellos	aquellas	

- Demonstrative adjectives normally precede the noun and always agree in number and in gender (→1)

- The forms **ese/a/os/as** are used:
  - to indicate distance from the speaker but proximity to the person addressed (→2)
  - to indicate a not too remote distance (→3)

- The forms **aquel/la/los/las** are used to indicate distance, in space or time (→4)

1   **Este bolígrafo no escribe**
    This pen is not working
    Esa revista es muy mala
    That is a very bad magazine
    Aquella montaña es muy alta
    That mountain (over there) is very high
    ¿Conoces a esos señores?
    Do you know those gentlemen?
    Siga Vd. hasta aquellos edificios
    Carry on until you come to those buildings
    ¿Ves aquellas personas?
    Can you see those people (over there)?

2   **Ese papel en donde escribes ...**
    That paper you are writing on ...

3   **No me gustan esos cuadros**
    I don't like those pictures

4   **Aquella calle parece muy ancha**
    That street (over there) looks very wide
    Aquellos años sí que fueron felices
    Those were really happy years

Interrogative Adjectives

	MASCULINE	FEMININE	
SING.	¿qué?	¿qué?	what?, which?
	¿cuánto?	¿cuánta?	how much?; how many?
PLUR.	¿qué?	¿qué?	what?, which?
	¿cuántos?	¿cuántas?	how much?; how many?

- Interrogative adjectives, when not invariable, agree in number and gender with the noun (→1)

- The forms shown above are also used in indirect questions (→2)

Exclamatory Adjectives

	MASCULINE	FEMININE	
SING.	¡qué!	¡qué!	what (a)
	¡cuánto!	¡cuánta!	what (a lot of)
PLUR.	¡qué!	¡qué!	what
	¡cuántos!	¡cuántas!	what (a lot of)

- Exclamatory adjectives, when not invariable, agree in number and gender with the noun (→3)

1   **¿Qué libro te gustó más?**
    Which book did you like most?
    ¿Qué clase de hombre es?
    What type of man is he?
    ¿Qué instrumentos toca Vd.?
    What instruments do you play?
    ¿Qué ofertas ha recibido Vd.?
    What offers have you received?
    ¿Cuánto dinero te queda?
    How much money have you got left?
    ¿Cuánta lluvia ha caído?
    How much rain have we had?
    ¿Cuántos vestidos quieres comprar?
    How many dresses do you want to buy?
    ¿Cuántas personas van a venir?
    How many people are coming?

2   **No sé a qué hora llegó**
    I don't know at what time she arrived
    Dígame cuántas postales quiere
    Tell me how many postcards you'd like

3   **¡Qué pena!**
    What a pity!
    ¡Qué tiempo tan/más malo!
    What lousy weather!
    ¡Cuánto tiempo!
    What a long time!
    ¡Cuánta pobreza!
    What poverty!
    ¡Cuántos autobuses!
    What a lot of buses!
    ¡Cuántas mentiras!
    What a lot of lies!

Possessive Adjectives

Weak forms

WITH SING. NOUN		WITH PLUR. NOUN		
MASC.	FEM.	MASC.	FEM.	
mi	mi	mis	mis	*my*
tu	tu	tus	tus	*your*
su	su	sus	sus	*his; her; its; your (of Vd.)*
nuestro	nuestra	nuestros	nuestras	*our*
vuestro	vuestra	vuestros	vuestras	*your*
su	su	sus	sus	*their; your (of Vds.)*

- All possessive adjectives agree in number and (when applicable) in gender with the noun, NOT WITH THE OWNER (→1)

- The weak forms always precede the noun (→1)

- Since the form **su(s)** can mean *his, her, your* (of **Vd., Vds.**) or *their*, clarification is often needed. This is done by adding **de él, de ella, de Vds.** etc. to the noun, and usually (but not always) changing the possessive to a definite article (→2)

Continued

1 **Pilar no ha traído nuestros libros**
   Pilar hasn't brought our books
   Antonio irá a vuestra casa
   Anthony will go to your house
   ¿Han vendido su coche tus vecinos?
   Have your neighbours sold their car?
   Mi hermano y tu primo no se llevan bien
   My brother and your cousin don't get on

2 **su casa → la casa de él**
   his house
   sus amigos → los amigos de Vd.
   your friends
   sus coches → los coches de ellos
   their cars
   su abrigo → el abrigo de ella
   her coat

Possessive Adjectives (ctd.)

Strong forms

WITH SING. NOUN		WITH PLUR. NOUN		
MASC.	FEM.	MASC.	FEM.	
mío	mía	míos	mías	my
tuyo	tuya	tuyos	tuyas	your
suyo	suya	suyos	suyas	his; her; its; your (of Vd.)
nuestro	nuestra	nuestros	nuestras	our
vuestro	vuestra	vuestros	vuestras	your
suyo	suya	suyos	suyas	their; your (of Vds.)

● The strong forms agree in the same way as the weak forms (see p. 216)

● The strong forms always follow the noun, and they are used:
  – to translate the English of mine, of yours, etc. (→1)
  – to address people (→2)

● The clarification of **suyo** is similar to that of **su** (see p. 216) (→3)

1 **Es un capricho suyo**
   It's a whim of hers
   un amigo nuestro
   a friend of ours
   una revista tuya
   a magazine of yours

2 **Muy señor mío** (in letters)
   Dear Sir
   hija mía
   my daughter
   ¡Dios mío!
   My God!
   Amor mío
   My love/Darling

3 **en la casa suya → en la casa de él**
   in his house
   con los parientes suyos → con los parientes de ella
   with her relatives

Indefinite Adjectives

alguno(a)s	some
ambos(as)	both
cada	each; every
cierto(a)s	certain; definite
cualquiera, plur. cualesquiera	some; any
los (las) demás	the others; the remainder
mismo(a)s	same; -self
mucho(a)s	many; much
ningún, ninguna	any; no
plur. ningunos, ningunas	
otro(a)s	other; another
poco(a)s	few; little
tal(es)	such (a)
tanto(a)s	so much; so many
todo(a)s	all; every
varios(as)	several; various

Unless invariable, all indefinite adjectives agree in number and gender with the noun (→1)

- **alguno**
  Before a masculine singular noun it drops the final -**o** and adds an accent to show the correct position for stress (→2) (see also p. 292)

- **ambos**
  Usually it is only used in written Spanish. The spoken language prefers the form **los dos/las dos** (→3)

- **cierto and mismo**
  They change their meaning according to their position in relation to the noun (see also **Position of Adjectives**, p. 224) (→4)

- **cualquiera**
  It drops the final -**a** before a masculine OR feminine noun (→5)

Continued

1 el mismo día   las mismas películas
    the same day   the same films
    mucha/poca gente   **mucho/poco dinero**
    many/few people   much/little money

2 algún día   alguna razón
    some day   some reason

3 Me gustan los dos cuadros
    I like both pictures
    ¿Conoces a las dos enfermeras?
    Do you know both nurses?

4 cierto tiempo   BUT   éxito cierto
    a certain time   sure success
    el mismo color   BUT   en la iglesia misma
    the same colour   in the church itself

5 cualquier casa   BUT   una revista cualquiera
    any house   any magazine

Indefinite Adjectives (ctd.)

- **ningún** is only used in negative sentences or phrases (→1)

- **otro**
  It is never preceded by an indefinite article (→2)

- **tal**
  It is never followed by an indefinite article (→3)

- **todo**
  It must always be followed by a definite article, a demonstrative or possessive adjective or an object pronoun (→4)
  EXCEPTIONS:
  − when **todo** in the singular means *any, every*, or *each* (→5)
  − in some set expressions (→6)

1 No es ninguna tonta
She's no fool
¿No tienes parientes? No, ninguno
Haven't you any relatives? No, none

2 **¿Me das otra manzana?**
Will you give me another apple?
Prefiero estos otros zapatos
I prefer these other shoes.

3 **Nunca dije tal cosa**
I never said such a thing

4 **Estudian durante toda la noche**
They study all night
Ha llovido toda esta semana
It has rained all this week
Pondré en orden todos mis libros
I'll sort out all my books

5 **Podrá entrar toda persona que lo desee**
Any person who wishes to enter may do so
BUT
Vienen todos los días
They come every day

6 de todos modos
anyway
por todas partes
por todos lados $\left.\right\}$ everywhere
a/en todas partes
a/en todos lados

Position of Adjectives

- Spanish adjectives usually follow the noun (→1, 2)

- Note that when used figuratively or to express a quality already inherent in the noun, adjectives can precede the noun (→3)

- As in English, demonstrative, possessive (weak forms), numerical, interrogative and exclamatory adjectives precede the noun (→4)

- Indefinite adjectives also precede the noun usually (→5)
  But note that **alguno** some in negative expressions follows the noun (→6)

- Some adjectives can precede or follow the noun, but their meaning varies according to their position:

BEFORE NOUN		AFTER NOUN	
antiguo	former	old, ancient	(→7)
diferente	various	different	(→8)
grande	great	big	(→9)
medio	half	average	(→10)
mismo	same	-self, very/precisely	(→11)
nuevo	new, another, fresh	brand new	(→12)
pobre	poor (wretched)	poor (not rich)	(→13)
puro	sheer, mere	pure (clear)	(→14)
varios	several	various, different	(→15)
viejo	old (long known, etc.)	old (aged)	(→16)

- Adjectives following the noun are linked by **y**   (→17)

1 la página siguiente
  the following page

  la hora exacta
  the right time

2 una corbata azul
  a blue tie

  una palabra española
  a Spanish word

3 un dulce sueño
  a sweet dream
  un terrible desastre (all disasters are terrible)
  a terrible disaster

4 este sombrero
  this hat

  mi padre
  my father

  ¿qué hombre?
  what man?

5 cada día
  every day

  otra vez
  another time

  poco dinero
  little money

6 sin duda alguna
  without any doubt

7 un antiguo colega
  a former colleague

  la historia antigua
  ancient history

8 diferentes capítulos
  various chapters

  personas diferentes
  different people

9 un gran pintor
  a great painter

  una casa grande
  a big house

10 medio melón
   half a melon

   velocidad media
   average speed

11 la misma respuesta
   the same answer

   yo mismo   eso mismo
   myself   precisely that

12 mi nuevo coche
   my new car

   unos zapatos nuevos
   (some) brand new shoes

13 esa pobre mujer
   that poor woman

   un país pobre
   a poor country

14 la pura verdad
   the plain truth

   aire puro
   fresh air

15 varios caminos
   several ways/paths

   artículos varios
   various items

16 un viejo amigo
   an old friend

   esas toallas viejas
   those old towels

17 una acción cobarde y falsa
   a cowardly, deceitful act

Personal Pronouns

	SUBJECT PRONOUNS	
PERSON	SINGULAR	PLURAL
1st	yo	nosotros
	I	*we (masc./masc. + fem.)*
		nosotras
		we (all fem.)
2nd	tú	vosotros
	you	*you (masc./masc. + fem.)*
		vosotras
		you (all fem.)
3rd	él	ellos
	he; it	*they (masc./masc. + fem.)*
	ella	ellas
	she; it	*they (all fem.)*
	usted (Vd.)	ustedes (Vds.)
	you	*you*

- Subject pronouns have a limited usage in Spanish. Normally they are only used:
  - for emphasis (→1)
  - for clarity (→2)
  EXCEPTIONS: **Vd.** and **Vds.** should always be used for politeness, whether they are otherwise needed or not (→3)
- *It* as subject and *they*, referring to things, are never translated into Spanish (→4)
- tú/usted
  As a general rule, you should use **tú** (or **vosotros**, if plural) when addressing a friend, a child, a relative, someone you know well, or when invited to do so. In all other cases, use **usted** (or **ustedes**)
- nosotros/as; vosotros/as; él/ella; ellos/ellas
  All these forms reflect the number and gender of the noun(s) they replace. **Nosotros, vosotros** and **ellos** also replace a combination of masculine and feminine nouns.

Continued

1 **Ellos sí que llegaron tarde**
   They really did arrive late
   Tú no tienes por qué venir
   There is no reason for you to come
   Ella jamás creería eso
   She would never believe that

2 **Yo estudio español pero él estudia francés**
   I study Spanish but he studies French
   Ella era muy deportista pero él prefería jugar a las cartas
   She was a sporty type but he preferred to play cards
   Vosotros saldréis primero y nosotros os seguiremos
   You leave first and we will follow you

3 **Pase Vd. por aquí**
   Please come this way
   ¿Habían estado Vds. antes en esta ciudad?
   Had you been to this town before?

4 **¿Qué es? — Es una sorpresa**
   What is it? — It's a surprise
   ¿Qué son? — Son abrelatas
   What are they? — They are can-openers

Personal Pronouns (ctd.)

	DIRECT OBJECT PRONOUNS	
PERSON	SINGULAR	PLURAL
1st	**me**	**nos**
	me	*us*
2nd	**te**	**os**
	you	*you*
3rd (masculine)	**lo**	**los**
	him; it; you	*them; you*
	(of Vd.)	*(of Vds.)*
(feminine)	**la**	**las**
	her; it; you	*them; you*
	(of Vd.)	*(of Vds.)*

- lo sometimes functions as a 'neuter' pronoun, referring to an idea or information contained in a previous statement or question. It is often not translated (→1)

Position of direct object pronouns

- In constructions other than the imperative affirmative, infinitive or gerund, the pronoun always comes before the verb (→2)
  In the imperative affirmative, infinitive and gerund, the pronoun follows the verb and is attached to it. An accent is needed in certain cases to show the correct position for stress (see also p. 292) (→3)
- Where an infinitive or gerund depend on a previous verb, the pronoun may be used either after the infinitive or gerund, or before the main verb (→4)
  Note how this applies to reflexive verbs (→4)
- For further information, see Order of Object Pronouns, p. 232

Reflexive Pronouns

These are dealt with under reflexive verbs, p. 24.
Continued

1 **¿Va a venir María? — No lo sé**
Is María coming? — I don't know
Hay que regar las plantas — Yo lo haré
The plants need watering — I'll do it
Habían comido ya pero no nos lo dijeron
They had already eaten, but they didn't tell us
Yo conduzco de prisa pero él lo hace despacio
I drive fast but he drives slowly

2 **Te quiero**
I love you
¿Las ve Vd.?
Can you see them?
¿No me oyen Vds.?
Can't you hear me?
Tu hija no nos conoce
Your daughter doesn't know us
No los toques
Don't touch them

3 **Ayúdame**   **Acompáñenos**
Help me   Come with us
Quiero decirte algo
I want to tell you something
Estaban persiguiéndonos
They were coming after us

4 **Lo está comiendo OR Está comiéndolo**
She is eating it
Nos vienen a ver OR Vienen a vernos
They are coming to see us
No quería levantarse OR No se quería levantar
He didn't want to get up
Estoy afeitándome OR Me estoy afeitando
I'm shaving

Personal Pronouns (ctd.)

INDIRECT OBJECT PRONOUNS

PERSON	SINGULAR	PLURAL
1st	**me**	**nos**
2nd	**te**	**os**
3rd	**le**	**les**

- The pronouns shown in the above table replace the preposition **a** + noun (→**1**)

Position of indirect object pronouns

- In constructions other than the imperative affirmative, the infinitive or the gerund, the pronoun comes before the verb (→**2**)
  In the imperative affirmative, infinitive and gerund, the pronoun follows the verb and is attached to it. An accent is needed in certain cases to show the correct position for stress (see also p. 292) (→**3**)

- Where an infinitive or gerund depend on a previous verb, the pronoun may be used either after the infinitive or gerund, or before the main verb (→**4**)

- For further information, see Order of Object Pronouns, p. 232.

Reflexive Pronouns

These are dealt with under reflexive verbs, p. 24

Continued

1 **Estoy escribiendo a Teresa** → **Le estoy escribiendo**
I am writing to Teresa   I am writing to her
   Da de comer al gato   → **Dale de comer**
   Give the cat some food   Give it some food

2 **Sofía os ha escrito**   **¿Os ha escrito Sofía?**
Sophie has written to you   Has Sophie written to you?
   Carlos no nos habla
   Charles doesn't speak to us
   ¿Qué te pedían?
   What were they asking you for?
   No les haga caso Vd.
   Don't take any notice of them

3 **Respóndame Vd.**   **Díganos Vd. la respuesta**
Answer me   Tell us the answer
   No quería darte la noticia todavía
   I didn't want to tell you the news yet
   Llegaron diciéndome que ...
   They came telling me that ...

4 **Estoy escribiéndole OR Le estoy escribiendo**
I am writing to him/her
   Les voy a hablar OR Voy a hablarles
   I'm going to talk to them

Personal Pronouns (ctd.)

Order of object pronouns

- When two object pronouns of different persons are combined, the order is: indirect before direct, i.e.

me			lo	
te	}	before	la	
nos			los	(→1)
os			las	

  Note: When two 3rd person object pronouns are combined, the first (i.e. the indirect object pronoun) becomes **se** (→2)

Points to note on object pronouns

- As le/les can refer to either gender, and **se** to either gender, singular or plural, sometimes clarification is needed. This is done by adding **a él** *to him*, **a ella** *to her*; **a Vd.** *to you* etc. to the phrase, usually after the verb (→3)

- When a noun object precedes the verb, the corresponding object pronoun must be used too (→4)

- Indirect object pronouns are often used instead of possessive adjectives with parts of the body or clothing to indicate 'ownership', and also in certain common constructions involving reflexive verbs (see also **The Indefinite Article**, p. 198) (→5)

- **Le** and **les** are often used in Spanish instead of **lo** and **los** when referring to people. Equally **la** is sometimes used instead of **le** when referring to a feminine person or animal, although this usage is less frequent (→6)

Continued

1 **Paloma os lo mandará mañana**
Paloma is sending it to you tomorrow
¿Te los ha enseñado mi hermana?
Has my sister shown them to you?
No me lo digas
Don't tell me (that)
Todos estaban pidiéndotelo
They were all asking you for it
No quiere prestárnosla
He won't lend it to us

2 **Se lo di ayer**
I gave it to him/her/them yesterday

3 **Le escriben mucho a ella**
They write to her often
Se lo van a mandar pronto a ellos
They will be sending it to them soon

4 **A tu hermano lo conozco bien**
I know your brother well
A María la vemos algunas veces
We sometimes see María

5 **La chaqueta le estaba ancha**
His jacket was too loose
Me duele el tobillo
My ankle is aching
Se me ha perdido el bolígrafo
I have lost my pen

6 **Le/lo encontraron en el cine**
They met him at the cinema
Les/los oímos llegar
We heard them coming
Le/la escribimos una carta
We wrote a letter to her

Personal Pronouns (ctd.)

Pronouns after prepositions

- These are the same as the subject pronouns, except for the forms **mí** *me*, **tí** *you* (sing.), and the reflexive **sí** *himself, herself, themselves, yourselves* (→1)

- **Con** *with* combines with **mí**, **tí** and **sí** to form
  conmigo *with me*   (→2)
  contigo *with you*
  consigo *with himself/herself* etc.

- The following prepositions always take a subject pronoun:
entre	*between, among* (→3)
hasta **incluso** }	*even, including* (→4)
salvo **menos** }	*except* (→5)
según	*according to* (→6)

- These pronouns are used for emphasis, especially where contrast is involved (→7)

- **Ello** *it, that* is used after a preposition when referring to an idea already mentioned, but never to a concrete noun (→8)

- **A él**, **de él** NEVER contract (→9)

1 **Pienso en tí**
   I think about you
   Es para ella
   This is for her
   Volveréis sin nosotros
   You'll come back without us
   Hablaba para sí
   He was talking to himself

   ¿Son para mí?
   Are they for me?
   Iban hacia ellos
   They were going towards them
   Volaban sobre vosotros
   They were flying above you

2 **Venid conmigo**
   Come with me
   Lo trajeron consigo
   They brought it/him with them

   BUT   **¿Hablaron con vosotros?**
         Did they talk to you?

3 **entre tú y ella**
   between you and her

4 **Hasta yo puedo hacerlo**
   Even I can do it

5 **todos menos yo**
   everybody except me

6 **según tú**
   according to you

7 **¿A tí no te escriben?**
   Don't they write to you?
   Me lo manda a mí, no a tí
   She is sending it to me, not to you

8 **Nunca pensaba en ello**
   He never thought about it
   Por todo ello me parece que ...
   For all those reasons it seems to me that ...

9 **A él no lo conozco**
   I don't know him

   No he sabido nada de él
   I haven't heard from him

Indefinite Pronouns

algo	something, anything	(→1)
alguien	somebody, anybody	(→2)
alguno/a/os/as	some, a few	(→3)
cada uno/a	each (one) everybody	(→4)
cualquiera	anybody; any	(→5)
los/las demás	the others the rest	(→6)
mucho/a/os/as	many; much	(→7)
nada	nothing	(→8)
nadie	nobody	(→9)
ninguno/a	none, not any	(→10)
poco/a/os/as	few; little	(→11)
tanto/a/os/as	so much; so many	(→12)
todo/a/os/as	all; everything	(→13)
uno ... (el) otro una ... (la) otra }	(the) one ... the other	
unos ... (los) otros unas ... (las) otras }	some ... (the) others	(→14)
varios/as	several	(→15)

- algo, alguien, alguno

They can never be used after a negative. The appropriate negative pronouns are used instead: **nada, nadie, ninguno** (see also negatives, p. 272) (→16)

1   **Tengo algo para tí**   **¿Viste algo?**
    I have something for you   Did you see anything?

2   **Alguien me lo ha dicho**   **¿Has visto a alguien?**
    Somebody said it to me   Have you seen anybody?

3   **Algunos de los niños ya sabían leer**
    Some of the children could read already

4   **Le dió una manzana a cada uno**   **¡Cada uno a su casa!**
    She gave each of them an apple   Everybody go home!

5   **Cualquiera puede hacerlo**
    Anybody can do it
    Cualquiera de las explicaciones vale
    Any of the explanations is a valid one

6   **Yo me fui, los demás se quedaron**
    I went, the others stayed

7   **Muchas de las casas no tenían jardín**
    Many of the houses didn't have a garden

8   **¿Qué tienes en la mano? — Nada**
    What have you got in your hand? — Nothing

9   **¿A quién ves? — A nadie**
    Who can you see? — Nobody

10 **¿Cuántas tienes? — Ninguna**
    How many have you got? — None

11 **Había muchos cuadros, pero vi pocos que me gustaran**
    There were many pictures, but I saw few I liked

12 **¿Se oía mucho ruido? — No tanto**
    Was it very noisy? — Not so very.

13 **Lo ha estropeado todo**   **Todo va bien**
    He has spoiled everything   All is going well

14 **Unos cuestan 300 pesetas, los otros 400 pesetas**
    Some cost 300 pesetas, the others 400 pesetas

15 **Varios de ellos me gustaron mucho**
    I liked several of them very much

16 **Veo a alguien**   **No veo a nadie**
    I can see somebody   I can't see anybody
    Tengo algo que hacer   **No tengo nada que hacer**
    I have something to do   I don't have anything to do

Relative Pronouns

PEOPLE

SINGULAR	PLURAL	
que	que	who, that (subject) (→1)
que	que	} who(m), that (direct object) (→2)
a quien	a quienes	
a quien	a quienes	to whom, that (→3)
de que	de que	
de quien	de quienes	} of whom, that (→4)
cuyo/a	cuyos/as	whose (→5)

THINGS

SINGULAR AND PLURAL		
que	which, that (subject)	(→6)
que	which, that (direct object)	(→7)
a que	to which, that	(→8)
de que	of which, that	(→9)
cuyo	whose	(→10)

But note that these forms can also refer to people

- cuyo agrees with the noun it accompanies, NOT WITH THE OWNER (→5/10)

- You cannot omit the relative pronoun in Spanish as you can in English (→2/7)

Continued

1   **Mi hermano, que tiene veinte años, es el más joven**
My brother, who is twenty, is the youngest

2   **Los amigos que más quiero son ...**
The friends (that) I like best are ...
María, a quien admira Daniel, es ...
María, whom Daniel admires, is ...

3   **Mis padres, a quienes he escrito una carta, están ...**
My parents, to whom I've written a letter, are ...

4   **La chica de que te hablé llega mañana**
The girl (that) I told you about is coming tomorrow
los niños de quienes se ocupa Vd.
the children (that) you look after

5   **Vendrá la mujer cuyo hijo está enfermo**
The woman whose son is ill will be coming

6   **Hay una escalera que lleva a la buhardilla**
There's a staircase which leads to the loft

7   **La casa que hemos comprado tiene ...**
The house (which) we've bought has ...
Este es el regalo que me ha mandado mi amiga
This is the present (that) my friend has sent to me

8   **la tienda a que siempre va**
the shop (which) she always goes to

9   **las injusticias de que se quejan**
the injustices (that) they're complaining about

10   **la ventana cuyas cortinas están corridas**
the window whose curtains are drawn

Relative Pronouns (ctd.)

el cual, el que

- These are used when the relative is separated from the word it refers to, or when it would otherwise be unclear which word it referred to. The pronouns always agree in number and gender with the noun (→1)
  El cual may also be used when the verb in the relative clause is separated from the relative pronoun (→2)

lo que, lo cual

- The neuter form lo is normally used when referring to an idea, statement or abstract noun. In certain expressions, the form lo cual may also be used (→3)

Relative pronouns after prepositions

- **Que** and **quienes** are generally used after the prepositions:

a	to (→4)
con	with (→5)
de	from, about, of (→6)
en	in, on, into (→7)

  It should be noted that **en que** can sometimes be translated by:
  - *where*. In this case it can also be replaced by **en donde** or **donde** (→8)
  - *when*. Sometimes here it can be replaced by **cuando** (→9)

- **El que** or **el cual** are used after other prepositions, and they always agree (→10)

Continued

1   **El padre de Elena, el cual tiene mucho dinero, es ...**
    Elena's father, who has a lot of money, is ...
    (**el cual** is used here since **que** or **quien** might equally refer
    to Elena)
    **Las plantas del vecino, las cuales/las que siempre está
    regando ...**
    The neighbour's plants, which he is always watering ...

2   **Vieron a su tío, el cual, después de levantarse, salió**
    They saw their uncle, who, after having got up, went out

3   **No sabe lo que hace**
    He doesn't know what he is doing
    Lo que dijiste fue una tontería
    What you said was foolish
    **Todo estaba en silencio, lo que (or lo cual) me pareció
    muy raro**
    All was silent, which I thought most odd

4   **las tiendas a que íbamos**
    the shops we used to go to

5   **la chica con quien sale**
    the girl he's going out with

6   **el libro de que te hablé**
    the book I told you about

7   **el lío en que te has metido**
    the trouble you've got yourself into

8   **el sitio en que (en donde/donde) se escondía**
    the place where he/she was hiding

9   **el año en que naciste**
    the year (when) you were born

10 **el puente debajo del que/cual pasa el río**
    the bridge under which the river flows
    las obras por las cuales/que es famosa
    the plays for which she is famous

Relative Pronouns (ctd.)

el que, la que; los que, las que

These mean *the one(s) who/which, those who* (→**1**)
Note that **quien(es)** can replace **el que** *etc* when used in a general sense (→**2**)

todos los que, todas las que

These mean *all who, all those/the ones which* (→**3**)

todo lo que

This translates *all that, everything that* (→**4**)

el de, la de; los de, las de

These can mean:
— *the one(s) of, that/those of* (→**5**)
— *the one(s) with* (→**6**)

1 **Esa película es la que quiero ver**
That film is the one I want to see
¿Te acuerdas de ese amigo? El que te presenté ayer
Do you remember that friend? The one I introduced you to
yesterday
Los que quieran entrar tendrán que pagar
Those who want to go in will have to pay

2 **Quien (or el que) llegue antes ganará el premio**
He who arrives first will win the prize

3 **Todos los que salían iban de negro**
All those who were coming out were dressed in black
**¿Qué autobuses puedo tomar? — Todos los que pasen por
aquí**
Which buses can I take? — Any (All those) that come this way

4 **Quiero saber todo lo que ha pasado**
I want to know all that has happened

5 **Trae la foto de tu novio y la de tu hermano**
Bring the photo of your boyfriend and the one of your brother
Viajamos en mi coche y el de María
We travelled in my car and Maria's
Te doy estos libros y también los de mi hermana
I'll give you these books and my sister's too

6 **Tu amigo, el de las gafas, me lo contó**
Your friend, the one with glasses, told me

Interrogative Pronouns

¿qué?   *what?; which?*
¿cuál(es)? *which?; what?*
¿quién(es)? *who?*

qué

It always translates *what* (→**1**)
Note, however, that **por** + **qué** is normally translated by *why*
(→**2**)

cuál

It normally implies a choice, and translates *which* (→**3**) EXCEPT
when no choice is implied or more specific information is
required (→**4**)

quién

— **quién(es)** (subject or after preposition)   *who*   (→**5**)
— **a quién(es)** (object)   *whom* (→**6**)
— **de quién(es)**   *whose* (→**7**)

- All the forms shown above are also used in indirect questions
(→**8**)

1 **¿Qué estan haciendo?**
What are they doing?
¿Qué dices?
What are you saying?
¿Para qué lo quieres?
What do you want it for?

2 **¿Por qué no llegaron Vds. antes?**
Why didn't you arrive earlier?

3 **¿Cuál de estos vestidos te gusta más?**
Which of these dresses do you like best?
¿Cuáles viste?
Which ones did you see?

4 **¿Cuál es la capital de España?**
What is the capital of Spain?
¿Cuál es tu consejo?
What is your advice?
¿Cuál es su fecha de nacimiento?
What is your date of birth?

5 **¿Quién ganó la carrera?**
Who won the race?
¿Con quiénes les viste?
Who did you see them with?

6 **¿A quiénes ayudaste?**
Who(m) did you help?
¿A quién se lo diste?
Who did you give it to?

7 **¿De quién es este libro?**
Whose is this book?

8 **Le pregunté para qué lo quería**
I asked him/her what he/she wanted it for
No me dijeron cuáles preferían
They didn't tell me which ones they preferred
No sabía a quién acudir
I didn't know who to turn to

Possessive Pronouns

These are the same as the strong forms of the possessive adjectives, but they are always accompanied by the definite article.

SINGULAR

MASCULINE	FEMININE	
el mío	la mía	*mine*
el tuyo	la tuya	*yours* (of tú)
el suyo	la suya	*his; hers; its; yours* (of **Vd.**)
el nuestro	la nuestra	*ours*
el vuestro	la vuestra	*yours* (of vosotros)
el suyo	la suya	*theirs; yours* (of **Vds.**)

PLURAL

MASCULINE	FEMININE	
los míos	las mías	*mine*
los tuyos	las tuyas	*yours* (of tú)
los suyos	las suyas	*his; hers; its; yours* (of **Vd.**)
los nuestros	las nuestras	*ours*
los vuestros	las vuestras	*yours* (of vosotros)
los suyos	las suyas	*theirs; yours* (of **Vds.**)

● The pronoun agrees in number and gender with the noun it replaces, NOT WITH THE OWNER (→1)

● Alternative translations are *my own, your own*, etc. (→2)

● After the prepositions a and de the article el is contracted in the normal way (see p. 196)

    a + el mío → al mío (→3)
    de + el mío → del mío (→4)

1   **Pregunta a Cristina si este bolígrafo es el suyo**
     Ask Christine if this pen is hers
     ¿Qué equipo ha ganado, el suyo o el nuestro?
     Which team won — theirs or ours?
     Mi perro es más joven que el tuyo
     My dog is younger than yours
     Daniel pensó que esos libros eran los suyos
     Daniel thought those books were his
     Si no tienes discos, te prestaré los míos
     If you don't have any records, I'll lend you mine
     Las habitaciones son menos amplias que las vuestras
     The rooms are smaller than yours

2   **¿Es su familia tan grande como la tuya?**
     Is his/her/their family as big as your own?
     Sus precios son más bajos que los nuestros
     Their prices are lower than our own

3   **¿Por qué prefieres este sombrero al mío?**
     Why do you prefer this hat to mine?
     Su coche se parece al vuestro
     His/her/their car looks like yours

4   **Mi libro está encima del tuyo**
     My book is on top of yours
     Su padre vive cerca del nuestro
     His/her/their father lives near ours

Demonstrative Pronouns

	MASCULINE	FEMININE	NEUTER	
SING.	éste	ésta	esto	*this*
	ése	ésa	eso	*that*
	aquél	aquélla	aquello	
PLUR.	éstos	éstas		*these*
	ésos	ésas		*those*
	aquéllos	aquéllas		

- The pronoun agrees in number and gender with the noun it replaces (→1)

- The difference in meaning between the forms **ése** and **aquél** is the same as between the corresponding adjectives (see p. 212)

- The masculine and feminine forms have an accent, which is the only thing that differentiates them from the corresponding adjectives.

- The neuter forms always refer to an idea, statement, etc., but never to specified nouns (→2)

- An additional meaning of **aquél** is the former, and of **éste** the latter (→3)

1 **¿Qué abrigo te gusta más? — Este de aquí**
   Which coat do you like best? — This one here
   Aquella casa era más grande que ésta
   That house was bigger than this one
   estos libros y aquéllos
   these books and those (over there)
   Quiero estas sandalias y ésas
   I'd like these sandals and those ones

2 **No puedo creer que esto me esté pasando a mí**
   I can't believe this is really happening to me
   Eso de madrugar es algo que no le gusta
   (This business of) getting up early is something she doesn't like
   Aquello sí que me gustó
   I really did like that

3 **Hablaban Jaime y Andrés, éste a voces y aquél casi en un susurro**
   James and Andrew were talking, the latter in a loud voice and the former almost in a whisper

Adverbs

Formation

- Most adverbs are formed by adding **-mente** to the feminine form of the adjective. Accents on the adjective are not affected since the suffix **-mente** is stressed independently (→1)
  Note, however, that **-mente** is omitted:
  - In the last of two or more of these adverbs when joined by a conjunction (→2)
  - In **recientemente** *recently* when immediately preceding a past participle (→3). An accent is then needed on the last syllable (see p. 292)

- The following adverbs are formed in an irregular way:

bueno	→	**bien**
good		*well*
malo	→	**mal**
bad		*badly*

Adjectives used as adverbs

Certain adjectives are used adverbially. These include:
alto, bajo, barato, caro, claro, derecho, fuerte and **rápido** (→4)
It should be noted that other adjectives used as adverbs agree with the subject, and can normally be replaced by the adverb ending in **-mente** or an adverbial phrase (→5)

Position of Adverbs

- When the adverb accompanies a verb, it may either immediately follow it or precede it for emphasis (→6)
  Note, however, that the adverb can never be placed between **haber** and the past participle in compound tenses (→7)

- When the adverb accompanies an adjective or another adverb, it generally precedes the adjective or adverb (→8)

Continued

1 FEM. ADJECTIVE   ADVERB
  lenta slow   **lentamente** slowly
  franca frank   **francamente** frankly
  feliz happy   **felizmente** happily
  fácil easy   **fácilmente** easily

2 **Lo hicieron lenta pero eficazmente**
  They did it slowly but efficiently

3 **El pan estaba recién hecho**
  The bread had just been baked

4 **hablar alto/bajo**   **cortar derecho**
  to speak loudly/softly   to cut (in a) straight (line)
  costar barato/caro   **Habla muy fuerte**
  to be cheap/expensive   He talks very loudly
  ver claro   **correr rápido**
  to see clearly   to run fast

5 **Esperaban impacientes** (or **impacientemente/con impaciencia**)
  They were waiting impatiently
  Vivieron muy felices (or **muy felizmente**)
  They lived very happily
  La profesora habló severamente (or **con severidad**) **a sus alumnos**
  The teacher spoke to her pupils sternly

6 **No conocemos aún al nuevo médico**
  We still haven't met the new doctor
  Han hablado muy bien
  They have spoken very well
  Siempre le regalaban flores
  They always gave her flowers

7 **Lo he hecho ya**
  I've already done it
  No ha estado nunca en Italia
  She's never been to Italy

8 **un sombrero muy bonito**   **hablar demasiado alto**
  a very nice hat   to talk too loud
  mañana temprano   **hoy mismo**
  early tomorrow   today

Comparatives

These are formed using the following constructions:

más ... (que)	*more ... (than)*	(→1)
menos ... (que)	*less ... (than)*	(→2)
tanto como	*as much as*	(→3)
tan ... como	*as ... as*	(→4)
tan ... que	*so ... that*	(→5)
demasiado ...	*too ... to*	(→6)
(lo) bastante ... $\Big\}$ para	*enough to*	(→7)
(lo) suficientemente ...		
cada vez más/menos	*more and more/less and less*	(→8)

Superlatives

- These are formed by placing **más/menos** *the most/the least* before the adverb (→9)

- **lo** is added before a superlative which is qualified (→10)

- The absolute superlative (*very, most, extremely* + adverb) is formed by placing **muy** before the adverb. The form **-ísimo** (see also p. 292) is also occasionally found (→11)

Adverbs with irregular comparatives/superlatives

ADVERB	COMPARATIVE	SUPERLATIVE
bien	**mejor***	**(lo) mejor**
well	*better*	*(the) best*
mal	**peor**	**(lo) peor**
badly	*worse*	*(the) worst*
mucho	**más**	**(lo) más**
a lot	*more*	*(the) most*
poco	**menos**	**(lo) menos**
little	*less*	*(the) least*

* **más bien** also exists, meaning *rather* (→12)

Continued

1 **más de prisa**   **más abiertamente**
   more quickly   more openly
   Mi hermana canta más fuerte que yo
   My sister sings louder than me

2 **menos fácilmente**   **menos a menudo**
   less easily   less often
   Nos vemos menos frecuentemente que antes
   We see each other less frequently than before

3 **Daniel no lee tanto como Andrés**
   Daniel doesn't read as much as Andrew

4 **Hágalo tan rápido como le sea posible**
   Do it as quickly as you can
   Ganan tan poco como nosotros
   They earn as little as we do

5 **Llegaron tan pronto que tuvieron que esperarnos**
   They arrived so early that they had to wait for us

6 **Es demasiado tarde para ir al cine**
   It's too late to go to the cinema

7 **Eres (lo) bastante grande para hacerlo solo**
   You're old enough to do it by yourself

8 **Me gusta el campo cada vez más**
   I like the countryside more and more

9 **María es la que corre más rápido**
   Maria is the one who runs fastest
   El que llegó menos tarde fue Miguel
   Miguel was the one to arrive the least late

10 **Lo hice lo más de prisa que pude**
   I did it as quickly as I could

11 **muy lentamente   tempranísimo   muchísimo**
   very slowly   extremely early   very much

12 **Era un hombre más bien bajito**
   He was a rather short man
   Estaba más bien inquieta que impaciente
   I was restless rather than impatient

Common Adverbs and their usage

bastante	*enough; quite*	(→1)
bien	*well*	(→2)
cómo	*how*	(→3)
cuánto	*how much*	(→4)
demasiado	*too much; too*	(→5)
más	*more*	(→6)
menos	*less*	(→7)
mucho	*a lot; much*	(→8)
poco	*little, not much; not very*	(→9)
siempre	*always*	(→10)
también	*also, too*	(→11)
tan	*as*	(→12)
tanto	*as much*	(→13)
todavía/aún	*still; yet; even*	(→14)
ya	*already*	(→15)

● **bastante, cuánto, demasiado, mucho, poco** and **tanto** are also used as adjectives that agree with the noun they qualify (see indefinite adjectives, p. 220 and interrogative adjectives, p. 214)

1 **Es bastante tarde**
  It's quite late

2 **¡Bien hecho!**
  Well done!

3 **¡Cómo me ha gustado!**
  How I liked it!

4 **¿Cuánto cuesta este libro?**
  How much is this book?

5 **He comido demasiado**   **Es demasiado caro**
  I've eaten too much   It's too expensive

6 **Mi hermano trabaja más ahora** **Es más tímida que Sofía**
  My brother works more now   She is shyer than Sophie

7 **Se debe beber menos**   **Estoy menos sorprendida que tú**
  One must drink less   I'm less surprised than you are

8 **¿Lees mucho?**   **¿Está mucho más lejos?**
  Do you read a lot?   Is it much further?

9 **Comen poco**   **María es poco decidida**
  They don't eat (very) much   Maria is not very daring

10 **Siempre dicen lo mismo**
  They always say the same (thing)

11 **A mí también me gusta**
  I like it too

12 **Ana es tan alta como yo**
  Ana is as tall as I am

13 **Nos aburrimos tanto como vosotros**
  We got as bored as you did

14 **Todavía/aún tengo dos**   **Todavía/aún no han llegado**
  I've still got two   They haven't arrived yet
  Mejor aún/todavía
  Even better

15 **Ya lo he hecho**
  I've done it already

On the following pages you will find some of the most frequent uses of prepositions in Spanish. Particular attention is paid to cases where usage differs markedly from English. It is often difficult to give an English equivalent for Spanish prepositions, since usage *does* vary so much between the two languages. In the list below, the broad meaning of the preposition is given on the left, with examples of usage following. Prepositions are dealt with in alphabetical order, except **a**, **de**, **en** and **por** which are shown first.

a

at	echar algo a algn	to throw sth at sb
	a 50 pesetas el kilo	(at) 50 pesetas a kilo
	a 100 km por hora	at 100 km per hour
	sentarse a la mesa	to sit down at the table
in	al sol	in the sun
	a la sombra	in the shade
onto	cayeron al suelo	they fell onto the floor
	pegar una foto al álbum	to stick a photo into the album
to	ir al cine	to go to the cinema
	dar algo a algn	to give sth to sb
	venir a hacer	to come to do
from	quitar algo a algn	to take sth from sb
	robar algo a algn	to steal sth from sb
	arrebatar algo a algn	to snatch sth from sb
	comprar algo a algn	to buy sth from/for sb*
	esconder algo a algn	to hide sth from sb
means	a mano	by hand
	a caballo	on horseback (BUT note other forms of transport used with en and por)
	a pie	on foot

* The translation here obviously depends on the context

manner	a la inglesa	in the English manner
	a pasos lentos	with slow steps
	poco a poco	little by little
	a ciegas	blindly
time, date:	a medianoche	at midnight
at, on	a las dos y cuarto	at quarter past two
	a tiempo	on time
	a fines de mes	at the end of the month
	a veces	at times
distance	a 8 km de aquí	(at a distance of) 8 kms from here
	a dos pasos de mi casa	just a step from my house
	a lo lejos	in the distance
with el + infin.	al levantarse	on getting up
	al abrir la puerta	on opening the door
after certain adjectives	dispuesto a todo	ready for anything
	parecido a esto	similar to this
	obligado a ello	obliged to (do) that
after certain verbs	see p. 66	

Personal a

When the direct object of a verb is a person or pet animal, **a** must always be placed immediately before it.

EXAMPLES: **querían mucho a sus hijos**
they loved their children dearly
el niño miraba a su perro con asombro
the boy kept looking at his dog in astonishment

EXCEPTION: **tener**   **tienen dos hijos**
to have   *they have two children*

Continued

de

from	venir de Londres	to come from London
	un médico de Valencia	a doctor from Valencia
	de la mañana a la noche	from morning till night
	de 10 a 15	from 10 to 15
belonging to, of	el sombrero de mi padre	my father's hat
	las lluvias de abril	April showers
contents, composition, material	una caja de cerillas	a box of matches
	una taza de té	a cup of tea; a tea-cup
	un vestido de seda	a silk dress
destined for	una silla de cocina	a kitchen chair
	un traje de noche	an evening dress
descriptive	la mujer del sombrero verde	the woman with the green hat
	el vecino de al lado	the next door neighbour
manner	de manera irregular	in an irregular way
	de una puñalada	by stabbing
quality	una mujer de edad	an aged lady
	objetos de valor	valuable items
comparative + number	había más/menos de 100 personas	there were more/ fewer than 100 people
after superlatives: in	la ciudad más/menos bonita del mundo	the most/least beautiful city in the world
after certain adjectives	contento de ver	pleased to see
	fácil/difícil de entender	easy/difficult to understand
	capaz de hacer	capable of doing
after certain verbs	see p. 66	

after certain verbs see p. 66

en

in, at	en el campo	in the country
	en Londres	in London
	en la cama	in bed
	con un libro en la mano	with a book in his hand
	en voz baja	in a low voice
	en la escuela	in/at school
into	entra en la casa	go into the house
	metió la mano en su bolso	she put her hand into her handbag
on	un cuadro en la pared	a picture on the wall
	sentado en una silla	sitting on a chair
	en la planta baja	on the ground floor
time, dates, months: at, in	en este momento	at this moment
	en 1975	in 1975
	en enero	in January
transport: by	en coche	by car
	en avión	by plane
	en tren	by train (but see also por)
language	en español	in Spanish
duration	lo haré en una semana	I'll do it in one week
after certain adjectives	es muy buena/mala en geografía	she is very good/bad at geography
	fueron los primeros/ últimos/únicos en + infin.	they were the first/ last/only ones + infin.
after certain verbs	see p. 66	

Continued

por

motion: along, through, around	vaya por ese camino por el túnel pasear por el campo	go along that path through the tunnel to walk around the countryside
vague location	tiene que estar por aquí le busqué por todas partes	it's got to be somewhere around here I looked for him everywhere
vague time	por la tarde por aquellos días	in the afternoon in those days
rate	90 km por hora un cinco por ciento ganaron por 3 a 0	90 km per hour five per cent they won by 3 to 0
agent of passive: by	descubierto por unos niños odiado por sus enemigos	discovered by some children hated by his enemies
by (means of)	por barco por tren por correo aéreo llamar por teléfono	by boat by train (freight) by airmail to telephone
cause, reason: for, because	¿por qué? por todo eso por lo que he oído	why?, for what reason? because of all that judging by what I've heard
+ infinitive: to	libros por leer cuentas por pagar	books to be read bills to be paid
equivalence	¿me tienes por tonto?	do you think I'm stupid?
+ adjective/ adverb + que: however	por buenos que sean por mucho que lo quieras	however good they are however much you want it

por (ctd.)

for	¿cuanto me darán por este libro?	how much will they give me for this book?
	te lo cambio por éste	I'll swap you this one for it
	no siento nada por tí	I feel nothing for you
	si no fuera por tí	if it weren't for you
	¡Por Dios!	For God's sake!
for the benefit of	lo hago por ellos	I do it for their benefit
on behalf of	firma por mí	sign on my behalf

por also combines with other prepositions to form double prepositions usually conveying the idea of movement. The commonest of these are:

over	saltó por encima de la mesa	she jumped over the table
under	nadamos por debajo del puente	we swam under the bridge
past	pasaron por delante de Correos	they went past the Post Office
behind	por detrás de la puerta	behind the door
through	la luz entraba por entre las cortinas	light was coming in through the curtains
+ donde	¿por dónde has venido?	which way did you come?

ante

faced with, before	lo hicieron ante mis propios ojos	they did it before my very eyes
	ante eso no se puede hacer nada	one can't do anything when faced with that
preference	la salud ante todo	health above all things

antes de

before (time)	antes de las 5	before 5 o'clock

bajo/debajo de

These are usually equivalent, although **bajo** is used more frequently in a figurative sense and with temperatures.

under	**bajo/debajo de la cama**	under the bed
	bajo el dominio romano	under Roman rule
below	**un grado bajo cero**	one degree below zero

con

with	**vino con su amigo**	she came with her friend
after certain adjectives	**enfadado con ellos**	angry with them
	magnánimo con sus súbditos	magnanimous with his subjects

contra

| against | **no tengo nada contra ti** | I've nothing against you |
| | **apoyado contra la pared** | leaning against the wall |

delante de

| in front of | **iba delante de mí** | she was walking in front of me |

desde

from	**desde aquí se puede ver**	you can see it from here
	llamaban desde España	they were phoning from Spain
	desde otro punto de vista	from a different point of view
	desde la 1 hasta las 6	from 1 till 6
	desde entonces	from then onwards
since	**desde que volvieron**	since they returned
for	**viven en esa casa desde hace 3 años**	they've been living in that house for 3 years (NOTE TENSE)

detrás de

| behind | están detrás de la puerta | they are behind the door |

durante

| during | durante la guerra | during the war |
| for | anduvieron durante 3 días | they walked for 3 days |

entre

between	entre 8 y 10	between 8 and 10
among	María y Elena, entre otras	Maria and Elena, among others
reciprocal	ayudarse entre sí	to help each other

excepto

| except (for) | todos excepto tú | everybody except you |

hacia

towards	van hacia ese edificio	they're going towards that building
around (time)	hacia las 3	at around 3 (o'clock)
	hacia fines de enero	around the end of January

Hacia can also combine with some adverbs to convey a sense of motion in a particular direction:

hacia arriba	upwards
hacia abajo	downwards
hacia adelante	forwards
hacia atrás	backwards
hacia adentro	inwards
hacia afuera	outwards

Continued

hasta

until	hasta la noche	until night
as far as	viajaron hasta Sevilla	they travelled as far as Seville
up to	conté hasta 300 ovejas	I counted up to 300 lambs
	hasta ahora no los había visto	up to now I hadn't seen them
even	hasta un tonto lo entendería	even an imbecile would understand that

para

for	es para ti	it's for you
	es para mañana	it's for tomorrow
	un habitación para dos noches	a room for two nights
	para ser un niño, lo hace muy bien	for a child he is very good at it
	salen para Cádiz	they are leaving for Cádiz
	se conserva muy bien para sus años	he keeps very well for his age
+ infin.: (in order) to	es demasiado torpe para comprenderlo	he's too stupid to understand
+ sí: to oneself	hablar para sí	to talk to oneself
	reir para sí	to laugh to oneself
with time	todavía tengo para 1 hora	I'll be another hour (at it) yet

salvo

except (for)	todos salvo él	all except him
	salvo cuando llueve	except when it's raining
barring	salvo imprevistos	barring the unexpected
	salvo contraorden	unless you hear to the contrary

según

according to	según su consejo	according to her advice
	según lo que me dijiste	according to what you told me

sin

without	sin agua/dinero	without water/money
	sin mi marido	without my husband
+ infinitive	sin contar a los otros	without counting the others

sobre

on	sobre la cama	on the bed
	sobre el armario	on (top of) the wardrobe
on (to)	póngalo sobre la mesa	put it on the table
about, on	un libro sobre Eva Perón	a book about Eva Perón
above, over	volábamos sobre el mar	we were flying over the sea
	la nube sobre aquella montaña	the cloud above that mountain
approximately: about	vendré sobre las 4	I'll come about 4 o'clock
	Madrid tiene sobre 4 millones de habitantes	Madrid has about 4 million inhabitants

tras

behind	está tras el asiento	it's behind the seat
after	uno tras otro	one after another
	día tras día	day after day
	corrieron tras el ladrón	they ran after the thief

Conjunctions

There are conjunctions which introduce a main clause, such as **y** *and*, **pero** *but*, **si** *if*, **o** *or* etc., and those which introduce subordinate clauses like **porque** *because*, **mientras que** *while*, **después de que** *after* etc. They are used in much the same way as in English, but the following points are of note:

- Some conjunctions in Spanish require a following subjunctive, see pp. 60 to 63

- Some conjunctions are 'split' in Spanish like *both ... and*, *either ... or* in English:

tanto ... como	*both ... and*	(→**1**)
ni ... ni	*neither ... nor*	(→**2**)
o (bien) ... o (bien)	*either ... or (else)*	(→**3**)
sea ... sea	*either ... or*,	(→**4**)
	whether ... or	

- **y**
  - Before words beginning with **i-** or **hi-** + consonant it becomes **e** (→**5**)

- **o**
  - Before words beginning with **o-** or **ho-** it becomes **u** (→**6**)
  - Between numerals it becomes **ó** (→**7**)

- **que**
  - meaning *that* (→**8**)
  - in comparisons, meaning *that* (→**9**)
  - followed by the subjunctive, see p. 58

- **porque** (Not to be confused with **por qué** *why*)
  - **como** should be used instead at the beginning of a sentence (→**10**)

- **pero, sino**
  - **pero** normally translates *but* (→**11**)
  - **sino** is used when there is a direct contrast after a negative (→**12**)

1 **Estas flores crecen tanto en verano como en invierno**
These flowers grow in both summer and winter

2 **Ni él ni ella vinieron**
Neither he nor she came
No tengo ni dinero ni comida
I have neither money nor food

3 **Debe de ser o ingenua o tonta**
She must be either naïve or stupid
O bien me huyen o bien no me reconocen
Either they're avoiding me or else they don't recognize me

4 **Sea en verano, sea en invierno, siempre me gusta andar**
I always like walking, whether in summer or in winter

5 **Diana e Isabel**
Diana and Isabel
madre e hija   BUT   **árboles y hierba**
mother and daughter   trees and grass

6 **diez u once**   **minutos u horas**
ten or eleven   minutes or hours

7 **37 ó 38**
37 or 38

8 **Dicen que te han visto**
They say (that) they've seen you
¿Sabías que estábamos allí?
Did you know that we were there?

9 **Le gustan más que nunca**
He likes them more than ever
María es menos guapa que su hermana
Maria is less attractive than her sister

10 **Como estaba lloviendo no pudimos salir**
Because/As it was raining we couldn't go out
(Compare with: **No pudimos salir porque estaba lloviendo**)

11 **Me gustaría ir, pero estoy muy cansada**
I'd like to go, but I am very tired

12 **No es inglés sino escocés**
He is not English but Scottish

Augmentative, diminutive and pejorative suffixes

These can be used after nouns, adjectives and some adverbs. They are attached to the end of the word after any final vowel has been removed

e.g.   **puerta** → **puertita**
       doctor → **doctorcito**

Note however that further changes sometimes take place (see p. 296)

Augmentatives

These are used mainly to imply largeness, but they can also suggest clumsiness, ugliness or grotesqueness. The commonest augmentatives are:

     ón/ona   (→1)
     azo/a   (→2)
     ote/a   (→3)

Diminutives

These are used mainly to suggest smallness or to express a feeling of affection. Occasionally they can be used to express ridicule or contempt. The commonest diminutives are:

     ito/a   (→4)
     (e)cito/a   (→5)
     (ec)illo/a   (→6)
     (z)uelo/a   (→7)

Pejoratives

These are used to convey the idea that something is unpleasant or to express contempt. The commonest suffixes are:

     ucho/a   (→8)
     acho/a   (→9)
     uzo/a   (→10)
     uco/a   (→11)
     astro/a   (→12)

	ORIGINAL WORD	DERIVED FORM
1	un hombre a man	un hombrón a big man
2	bueno good	buenazo (person) easily imposed on
	un perro a dog	un perrazo a really big dog
	gripe flu	un gripazo a really bad bout of flu
3	grande big	grandote huge
	palabra word	palabrota swear word
	amigo friend	amigote old pal
4	una casa a house	una casita a cottage
	un poco a little	un poquito a little bit
	un rato a while	un ratito a little while
	mi hija my daughter	mi hijita my dear sweet daughter
	despacio slowly	despacito nice and slowly
5	un viejo an old man	un viejecito a little old man
	un pueblo a village	un pueblecito a small village
	una voz a voice	una vocecita a sweet little voice
6	una ventana a window	una ventanilla a small window (car, train etc)
	un chico a boy	un chiquillo a small boy
	una campana a bell	una campanilla a small bell
	un palo a stick	un palillo a toothpick
	un médico a doctor	un mediquillo a quack (doctor)
7	los pollos the chickens	los polluelos the little chicks
	hoyos hollows	hoyuelos dimples
	un ladrón a thief	un ladronzuelo a petty thief
	una mujer a woman	una mujerzuela a whore
8	un animal an animal	un animalucho a wretched animal
	un cuarto a room	un cuartucho a poky little room
	una casa a house	una casucha a shack
9	rico rich	ricacho nouveau riche
10	gente people	gentuza scum
11	una ventana a window	un ventanuco a miserable little window
12	un político a politician	un politicastro a 3rd-rate politician

Word order

Word order in Spanish is much more flexible than in English. You can often find the subject placed after the verb or the object before the verb, either for emphasis or for stylistic reasons (→1) There are some cases, however, where the order is always different from English. Most of these have already been dealt with under the appropriate part of speech, but are summarised here along with other instances not covered elsewhere.

- Object pronouns nearly always come before the verb (→2).
  For details, see pp. 228 to 231

- Qualifying adjectives nearly always come after the noun (→3).
  For details, see p. 224

- Following direct speech the subject always follows the verb (→4)

For word order in negative sentences, see p. 272
For word order in interrogative sentences, see p. 276

1 **Ese libro te lo di yo**
I gave you that book
No nos vio nadie
Nobody saw us

2 **Ya les veo**   **Me lo dieron ayer**
I can see them now   They gave it to me yesterday

3 **una ciudad española**   **vino tinto**
a Spanish town   red wine

4 — **Pienso que sí** — **dijo María**
'I think so', said Maria
— **No importa** — **replicó Daniel**
'It doesn't matter', Daniel replied

Negatives

A sentence is made negative by adding **no** between the subject and the verb (and any preceding object pronouns) (→1)

There are, however, some points to note:

— in phrases like *not her*, *not now*, etc. the Spanish **no** usually comes after the word it qualifies (→2)

— with verbs of saying, hoping, thinking etc. *not* is translated by **que no** (→3)

Double negatives

no ... nada	*nothing*	*(not ... anything)*
no ... nadie	*nobody*	*(not ... anybody)*
no ... más	*no longer*	*(not ... any more)*
no ... nunca	*never*	*(not ... ever)*
no ... jamás	*never (stronger)*	*(not ... ever)*
no ... más que	*only*	*(not ... more than)*
no ... ningún(o)(a)	*no*	*(not any)*
no ... tampoco	*not ... either*	
no ... ni ... ni	*neither ... nor*	
no ... ni siquiera	*not even*	

Word order

● **No** precedes the verb (and any object pronouns) in both simple and compound tenses, and the second element follows the verb (→4)

● **No** may never split two interdependent verbs (→4*)

● Sometimes the above negatives are placed before the verb (with the exception of **más** and **más que**), and **no** is then dropped (→5)

● For use of **nada, nadie** and **ninguno** as pronouns, see p. 236

Continued

1 AFFIRMATIVE   NEGATIVE

El coche es suyo   →   **El coche no es suyo**
The car is his   The car is not his
Yo me lo pondré   →   **Yo no me lo pondré**
I will put it on   I will not put it on

2 **¿Quién lo ha hecho? — Ella no**
Who did it? — Not her
¿Quieres un cigarrillo? — Ahora no
Do you want a cigarette? — Not now
Dame ese libro, el que está a tu lado no, el otro
Give me that book, not the one near you, the other one

3 **Opino que no**   **Dijeron que no**
I think not   They said not

4 **No dicen nada**
They don't say anything
No han visto a nadie
They haven't seen anybody
No me veréis más
You won't see me any more
No te olvidaré nunca/jamás
I'll never forget you
No habían recorrido más que 40 kms cuando …
They hadn't travelled more than 40 kms when …
No se me ha ocurrido ninguna idea
I haven't had any ideas
No quieren venir ellos tampoco*
They won't come either
No les estaban esperando ni mi hijo ni mi hija*
Neither my son nor my daughter were waiting for them

5 **Nadie ha venido hoy**
Nobody came today
Nunca me han gustado
I've never liked them
Ni mi hermano ni mi hermana fuman
Neither my brother nor my sister smokes

Negatives (ctd.)

Negatives in short replies

- **No**, *no* is the usual negative response to a question (→1)
  Note, however, that it is often translated as *not* (→2) (see also p. 272)

- Nearly all the other negatives listed on p. 272 may be used without a verb in a short reply (→3)

● Combinations of negatives

These are the most common combinations of negative particles:

no ... nunca más	(→4)
no ... nunca a nadie	(→5)
no ... nunca nada/nada nunca	(→6)
no ... nunca más que	(→7)
no ... ni ... nunca	(→8)

1 **¿Quieres venir con nosotros? — No**
   Do you want to come with us? — No

2 **¿Vienes o no?**
   Are you coming or not?

3 **¿Ha venido alguien? — ¡Nadie!**
   Has anyone come? — Nobody!
   ¿Has ido al Japón alguna vez? — Nunca
   Have you ever been to Japan? — Never

4 **No lo haré nunca más**
   I'll never do it again

5 **No se ve nunca a nadie por allí**
   You never see anybody around there

6 **No cambiaron nada nunca**
   They never changed anything

7 **No he hablado nunca más que con su mujer**
   I've only ever spoken to his wife

8 **No me ha escrito ni llamado por teléfono nunca**
   He/she has never written to me or phoned me

Question forms: direct

There are two ways of forming direct questions in Spanish:

- by inverting the normal word order so that
  subject + verb → verb + subject (→**1**)
- by maintaining the word order *subject + verb*, but by using a rising intonation at the end of the sentence (→**2**)

It should be noted that in compound tenses the auxiliary may never be separated from the past participle, as happens in English (→**3**)

Question forms: indirect

An indirect question is one that is 'reported', e.g. he asked me *what the time was*, tell me *which way to go*. Word order in indirect questions can adopt one of the two following patterns:

- interrogative word + subject + verb (→**4**)
- interrogative word + verb + subject (→**5**)

¿verdad?, ¿no?

These are used wherever English would use *isn't it?, don't they?, weren't we?, is it?* etc. tagged on to the end of a sentence (→**6**)

sí

Sí is the word for yes in answer to a question put either in the affirmative or in the negative (→**7**)

1 **¿Vendrá tu madre?**
Will your mother come?
¿Es posible eso?
Is it possible?

¿Lo trajo Vd.?
Did you bring it?
¿Cuándo volverán Vds.?
When will you come back?

2 **El gato, ¿se bebió toda la leche?**
Did the cat drink up all his milk?
Andrés, ¿va a venir?
Is Andrew coming?

3 **¿Lo ha terminado Vd.?**
Have you finished it?

¿Había llegado tu amigo?
Had your friend arrived?

4 **Dime qué autobuses pasan por aquí**
Tell me which buses come this way
No sé cuántas personas vendrán
I don't know how many people will turn up

5 **Me preguntó dónde trabajaba mi hermano**
He asked me where my brother worked
No sabemos a qué hora empieza la película
We don't know what time the film starts

6 **Hace calor, ¿verdad?**
It's warm, isn't it?
No se olvidará Vd., ¿verdad?
You won't forget, will you?
Estaréis cansados, ¿no?
You will be tired, won't you?
Te lo dijo María, ¿no?
Maria told you, didn't she?

7 **¿Lo has hecho? — Sí**
Have you done it? — Yes (I have)
¿No lo has hecho? — Si
Haven't you done it? — Yes (I have)

Beware of translating word by word. While on occasions this is quite possible, quite often it is not. The need for caution is illustrated by the following:

- English phrasal verbs (i.e. verbs followed by a preposition) e.g. *to run away*, *to fall down* are often translated by one word in Spanish (→1)

- English verbal constructions often contain a preposition where none exists in Spanish, or vice versa (→2)

- Two or more prepositions in English may have a single rendering in Spanish (→3)

- A word which is singular in English may be plural in Spanish, or vice versa (→4)

- Spanish has no equivalent of the possessive construction denoted by ...'s/...s' (→5)

Specific problems

-ing

This is translated in a variety of ways in Spanish:

- *to be ... -ing* can sometimes be translated by a simple tense (see also pp. 54 to 56) (→6)
  But, when a physical position is denoted, a past participle is used (→7)

- in the construction *to see/hear sb ... -ing*, use an infinitive (→8)

  -ing can also be translated by:
  — an infinitive (→9)
     (see p. 46)
  — a perfect infinitive (→10)
     (see p. 50)
  — a gerund (→11)
     (see p. 52)
  — a noun (→12)

Continued

1	huir	caerse	ceder
	to run away	to fall down	to give in
2	pagar	mirar	escuchar
	to pay for	to look at	to listen to
	encontrarse con	fijarse en	servirse de
	to meet	to notice	to use
3	extrañarse de		harto de
	to be surprised at		fed up with
	soñar con		contar con
	to dream of		to count on
4	unas vacaciones		sus cabellos
	a holiday		his/her hair
	la gente		mi pantalón
	people		my trousers
5	el coche de mi hermano		el cuarto de las niñas
	my brother's car		the children's bedroom
	(literally: . . . of my brother)		(literally: . . . of the children)
6	Se va mañana		¿Qué haces?
	He/she is leaving tomorrow		What are you doing?
7	Está sentado ahí		Estaba tendida en el suelo
	He is sitting over there		She was lying on the ground
8	Les veo venir		La he oído cantar
	I can see them coming		I've heard her singing
9	Me gusta ir al cine		¡Deja de hablar!
	I like going to the cinema		Stop talking!
	En vez de contestar		Antes de salir
	Instead of answering		Before leaving
10	Después de haber abierto la caja, María . . .		
	After opening the box, Maria . . .		
11	Pasamos la tarde fumando y charlando		
	We spent the afternoon smoking and chatting		
12	El esquí me mantiene en forma		
	Skiing keeps me fit		

to be (See also Verbal Idioms, pp. 74 to 76)

● In set expressions, describing physical and emotional conditions, **tener** is used:

tener calor/frío	*to be warm/cold*
tener hambre/sed	*to be hungry/thirsty*
tener miedo	*to be afraid*
tener razón	*to be right*

● Describing the weather, e.g. *what's the weather like?, it's windy/sunny,* use **hacer** (→1)

● For ages, e.g. *he is 6,* use **tener** (see also p. 306) (→2)

there is/there are

● Both are translated by **hay** (→3)

can, be able

● Physical ability is expressed by **poder** (→4)

● If the meaning is *to know how to,* use **saber** (→5)

● *Can* + a 'verb of hearing or seeing etc.' in English is not translated in Spanish (→6)

to

● Generally translated by **a** (→7)

● In time expressions, e.g. *10 to 6,* use **menos** (→8)

● When the meaning is *in order to,* use **para** (→9)

● Following a verb, as in *to try to do, to like to do,* see pp. 46 and 48

● *easy/difficult/impossible etc. to do* are translated by **fácil/ difícil/imposible** etc. **de hacer** (→10)

1 ¿Qué tiempo hace? **Hace bueno/malo/viento**
What's the weather like? It's lovely/miserable/windy

2 ¿Cuántos años tienes? **Tengo quince (años)**
How old are you? I'm fifteen

3 Hay un señor en la puerta
There's a gentleman at the door
Hay cinco libros en la mesa
There are five books on the table

4 No puedo salir contigo
I can't go out with you

5 ¿Sabes nadar?
Can you swim?

6 No veo nada ¿Es que no me oyes?
I can't see anything Can't you hear me?

7 Dale el libro a Isabel
Give the book to Isabel

8 las diez menos cinco a las siete menos cuarto
five to ten at a quarter to seven

9 Lo hice para ayudaros
I did it to help you
Se inclinó para atarse el cordón de zapato
He bent down to tie his shoe-lace

10 Este libro es fácil/difícil de leer
This book is easy/difficult to read

must

- When *must* expresses an assumption, **deber de** is often used (→1)
  Note, however, that this meaning is also often expressed by **deber** directly followed by the infinitive (→2)

- When it expresses obligation, there are three possible translations:
  - **tener que**   (→3)
  - **deber**   (→4)
  - **hay que** (impersonal)   (→5)

may

- If *may* expresses possibility, it can be translated by:
  - **poder**
  - **puede (ser) que** + subjunctive } (→6)

- To express permission, use **poder** (→7)

will

- If *will* expresses willingness or desire rather than the future, the present tense of **querer** is used (→8)

would

- If *would* expresses willingness, use the preterite or imperfect of **querer** (→9)

- When a repeated or habitual action in the past is referred to, use
  - the imperfect (→10)
  - the imperfect of **soler** + infinitive (→11)

1 **Ha debido de mentir**
He must have lied
Debe de gustarle
She must like it

2 **Debe estar por aquí cerca**
It must be near hear
Debo haberlo dejado en el tren
I must have left it on the train

3 **Tenemos que salir temprano mañana**
We must leave early tomorrow
Tengo que irme
I must go

4 **Debo visitarles**
I must visit them
Debéis escuchar lo que se os dice
You must listen to what is said to you

5 **Hay que entrar por ese lado**
One (We *etc*) must get in that way

6 **Todavía puede cambiar de opinion**
He may still change his mind
Creo que puede llover esta tarde
I think it may rain this afternoon
Puede (ser) que no lo sepa
She may not know

7 **¿Puedo irme?**   **Puede sentarse**
May I go?   You may sit down

8 **¿Quiere Vd. esperar un momento, por favor?**
Will you wait a moment, please?
No quiere ayudarme
He won't help me

9 **No quisieron venir**
They wouldn't come

10 **Las miraba hora tras hora**
She would watch them for hours on end

11 **Ultimamente solía comer muy poco**
Latterly he would eat very little

Pronunciation of Vowels

Spanish vowels are always clearly pronounced and not relaxed in unstressed syllables as happens in English.

EXAMPLES	HINTS ON PRONUNCIATION
[a] casa	Between English a as in *hat* and u as in *hut*
[e] pensar	Similar to English e in *pet*
[i] filo	Between English i as in *pin* and ee as in *been*
[o] loco	Similar to English o in *hot*
[u] luna	Between English ew as in *few* and u as in *put*

Pronunciation of Diphthongs

All these diphthongs are shorter than similar English diphthongs.

[ai] baile, hay	Like i in *side*
[au] causa	Like ou in *sound*
[ei] peine, rey	Like ey in *grey*
[eu] deuda	Like the vowel sounds in English *may you*, but without the sound of the y
[oi] boina, voy	Like oy in *boy*

Semi-consonants

[j] hacia, ya tiene, yeso labio, yo	i following a consonant and preceding a vowel, and y preceding a vowel are pronounced like English *yet*
[w] agua, bueno arduo, ruido	u following a consonant and preceding a vowel, is pronounced like English *walk* EXCEPTIONS **gue, gui** (see p. 286)

Pronunciation of Consonants

Some consonants are pronounced almost exactly as in English:
[l, m, n, f, k, and in some cases g]
Others, listed below, are similar to English, but differences
should be noted.

EXAMPLES

[p] padre [k] coco [t] tan	They are not aspirated, unlike English pot, cook and ten.
[t] todo, tú [d] doy, balde	Pronounced with the tip of the tongue touching the upper front teeth and not the roof of the mouth as in English.

The following consonants are not heard in English:

EXAMPLES

[β] labio	This is pronounced between upper and lower lips, which do not touch, unlike English b as in bend.
[ɣ] haga	Similar to English g as in gate, but tongue does not touch the soft palate.
[ɲ] año	Similar to ni in onion.
[x] jota	Like the guttural ch in loch
[r] pera	A single trill with the tip of the tongue against the teeth ridge.
[rr] rojo, perro	A multiple trill with the tip of the tongue against the teeth ridge.

From spelling to sounds

The pronunciation of the following letters and groups of letters should be noted.

LETTER	PRONOUNCED	
b, v	[b]	These letters have the same value. At the start of a breath group, and after written **m** and **n**, the sound is similar to English *boy* (→**1**)
	[β]	In all other positions, the sound is unknown in English (see p. 285) (→**2**)
c	[k]	Before **a, o, u** or a consonant, like English *keep* (→**3**)
	[θ/s]	Before **e, i** like English *thin*, or, in Latin America and parts of Spain, like English *same* (→**4**)
d	[d]	At the start of the breath group and after **l** or **n**, it is pronounced similarly to English *deep* (see p. 285) (→**5**)
	[ð]	Between vowels and after consonants (except **l** or **n**), it is pronounced very like English *though* (→**6**)
	[(ð)]	At the end of words, and in the verb ending **-ado**, it is often not pronounced (→**7**)
g	[x]	Before **e, i**, pronounced gutturally, similarly to English *loch* (→**8**)
	[g]	At the start of the breath group and after **n**, it is pronounced like English *get* (→**9**)
	[ɣ]	In other positions the sound is unknown in English (→**10**)
gue	[ge/ɣe]	The **u** is silent (→**11**)
gui	[gi/ɣi]	
güe	[gwe/ɣwe]	The **u** is pronounced like English *walk*
güi	[gwi/ɣwi]	(→**12**)

1 bomba   voy   vicio
   ['bomba]   [boi]   ['biθjo]

2 hubo   de veras   lavar
   ['uβo]   [de 'βeras]   [la'βar]

3 casa   coco   cumbre
   ['kasa]   ['koko]   ['kumbre]

4 cero   cinco
   ['θero/'sero] ['θiŋko/'siŋko]

5 doy   balde   bondad
   [doi]   ['balde]   [bon'dað]

6 modo   ideal
   ['moðo]   [iðe'al]

7 Madrid   comprado
   [ma'ðri(ð)]   [kom'pra(ð)o]

8 gente   giro   general
   ['xente]   ['xiro]   [xene'ral]

9 ganar   pongo
   [ga'nar]   ['poŋgo]

10 agua   agrícola
   ['aɣwa]   [a'ɣrikola]

11 guija   guerra   pague
   ['gixa]   ['gerra]   ['paɣe]

12 agüero   argüir
   [a'ɣwero]   [ar'ɣwir]

From spelling to sounds (ctd.)

h	[-]	This is always silent (→1)
j	[x]	Like the guttural sound in English loch, but often silent at the end of a word (→2)
ll	[ʎ]	Similar to the English -ll- in million (→3)
	[j/ʒ]	In some parts of Spain and in Latin America, like English yet or pleasure (→4)
-nv-	[mb]	This combination of letters is pronounced as in English imbibe (→5)
ñ	[ɲ]	As in English onion (→6)
q	[k]	Always followed by silent letter **u**, and pronounced as in English keep (→7)
s	[s]	Except where mentioned below, like English sing (→8)
	[z]	When followed by b, d, g, l, m, n like English zoo (→9)
y	[j]	Like English yes (→10)
	[dʒ]	In emphatic speech similar to English jam (→11)
	[ʒ]	In some parts of Latin America, like English leisure (→12)
x	[ks]	Between vowels, often like English exit (→13)
	[s]	Before a consonant, and, increasingly, even between vowels, like English send (→14)
z	[θ]	like English thin (→15)
	[s]	In some parts of Spain and in Latin America, like English send (→16)

1	**hombre** ['ombre]	**hoja** ['oxa]	**ahorrar** [ao'rrar]
2	**jota** ['xota]	**tejer** [te'xer]	**reloj** [re'lo(x)]
3	**calle** ['kaʎe]	**llamar** [ʎa'mar]	
4	**pillar** [pi'jar/pi'ʒar]	**olla** ['oja/'oʒa]	
5	**enviar** [em'bjar]	**sin valor** ['sim ba'lor]	
6	**uña** ['uɲa]	**bañar** [ba'ɲar]	
7	**aquel** [a'kel]	**querer** [ke'rer]	
8	**está** [es'ta]	**serio** ['serjo]	
9	**desde** ['dezðe]	**mismo** ['mizmo]	**asno** ['azno]
10	**yo** [jo]	**yedra** ['jeðra]	
11	**ya** [dʒa]	**yate** ['dʒate]	
12	**yeso** ['ʒeso]	**yerno** ['ʒerno]	
13	**éxito** ['eksito]	**máximo** ['maksimo]	
14	**extra** ['estra]	**sexto** ['sesto]	
15	**zapato** [θa'pato]	**zona** ['θona]	**luz** [luθ]
16	**zaguán** [sa'ɣwan]	**zueco** ['sweko]	**pez** [pes]

Normal Word Stress

There are simple rules to establish which syllable in a Spanish word is stressed. When an exception to these rules occurs an acute accent (stress-mark) is needed (see p. 292). These rules are as follows:

— words ending in a vowel or combination of vowels, or with the consonants -s or -n are stressed on the next to last syllable. The great majority of Spanish words fall into this category (→1)

— words ending in a consonant other than -s or -n bear the stress on the last syllable (→2)

— a minority of words bear the stress on the second to last syllable, and these always need an accent (→3)

— two nouns change their stress from singular to plural (→4)

Stress in diphthongs

In the case of diphthongs there are rules to establish which of the vowels is stressed (see p. 284 for pronunciation). These rules are as follows:

— diphthongs formed by the combination of a "weak" vowel (i, u) and a "strong" vowel (a, e or o) bear the stress on the strong vowel (→5)

— diphthongs formed by the combination of two "weak" vowels bear the stress on the second vowel (→6)

But note that two "strong" vowels don't form a diphthong but are pronounced as two separate vowels. In these cases stress follows the normal rules (→7)

1 casa — casas
house — houses
corre — corren
he runs — they run
palabra — palabras
word — words
crisis — crisis
crisis — crises

2 reloj
watch
verdad
truth
batidor
beater

3 murciélago
bat
pájaro
bird

4 carácter — caracteres
character — characters
régimen — regímenes
regime — regimes

5 baile
dance
boina — peine
beret — comb
causa — reina
cause — queen

6 fui — ruido
I went — noise

7 me mareo — caer
I feel dizzy — to fall
caos — correa
chaos — leash

The acute accent (´)

This is used in writing to show that a word is stressed contrary to the normal rules for stress (see p. 290) (→1)

The following points should be noted:

- The same syllable is stressed in the plural form of adjectives and nouns as in the singular. To show this it is necessary to:
  - add an accent to the last syllable of unaccented nouns and adjectives ending in -n (→2)
  - drop the accent from nouns and adjectives ending in -n or -s which have an accent on the last syllable (→3)

- The feminine form of accented nouns or adjectives does not have an accent (→4)

- When object pronouns are added to certain verb forms an accent is required to show that the syllable stressed in the verb form does not change. These verb forms are:
  - the gerund (→5)
  - the infinitive, when followed by two pronouns (→6)
  - imperative forms, except for the 2nd person plural (→7)

- The absolute superlative forms of adjectives are always accented (→8)

- Accents on adjectives are not affected by the addition of the adverbial suffix -mente (→9)

1	**autobús** bus		**revolución** revolution
	relámpago lightning		**árboles** trees
2	**orden** order	→	**órdenes** orders
	examen examination	→	**exámenes** examinations
	joven young	→	**jóvenes** young
3	**revolución** revolution	→	**revoluciones** revolutions
	autobús bus	→	**autobuses** buses
	parlanchín chatty	→	**parlanchines** chatty
4	**marqués** marquis	→	**marquesa** marchioness
	francés French (*masc.*)	→	**francesa** French (*fem.*)
5	**comprando** buying	→	**comprándo(se)lo** buying it (for him/her/them)
6	**vender** to sell	→	**vendérselas** to sell them to him/her/them
7	**compra** buy	→	**cómpralo** buy it
	hagan do	→	**háganselo** do it for him/her/them
8	**viejo** old	→	**viejísimo** ancient
	caro expensive	→	**carísimo** very expensive
9	**fácil** easy	→	**fácilmente** easily

The acute accent (ctd.)

It is also used to distinguish between the written forms of words which are pronounced the same but have a different meaning or function. These are as follows:

- Possessive adjectives/personal pronouns (→1)

- Demonstrative adjectives/demonstrative pronouns (→2)

- Interrogative and exclamatory forms of adverbs, pronouns and adjectives (→3)

  Note that the accent is used in indirect as well as direct questions and exclamations (→4)

- The pronoun él and the article el (→5)

- A small group of words which could otherwise be confused. These are:

de	of, from	dé	give (pres. subj.)
mas	but	más	more
si	if	sí	yes; himself etc. (→6)
solo/a	alone	sólo	only (→7)
te	you	té	tea

The dieresis (¨)

This is used only in the combinations güi or güe to show that the u is pronounced as a semi-consonant (see p. 284) (→8)

1 **Han robado mi coche**
   They've stolen my car
   ¿Te gusta tu trabajo?
   Do you like your job?

   A mí no me vio
   He didn't see me
   Tú, ¿que opinas?
   What do you think?

2 **Me gusta esta casa**
   I like this house
   ¿Ves aquellos edificios?
   Can you see those buildings

   Me quedo con ésta
   I'll take this one
   Aquéllos son más bonitos
   Those are prettier

3 **El chico con quien viajé**
   The boy I travelled with
   Donde quieras
   Wherever you want

   ¿Con quién viajste?
   Who did you travel with?
   ¿Dónde encontraste eso?
   Where did you find that?

4 **¿Cómo se abre?**
   How does it open

   No sé cómo se abre
   I don't know how it opens

5 **El puerto queda cerca**
   The harbour's nearby

   Él no quiso hacerlo
   HE refused to do it

6 **si no viene**
   if he doesn't come

   Sí que lo sabe
   Yes he DOES know

7 **Vino solo**
   He came by himself

   Sólo lo sabe él
   Only he knows

8 **¡Qué vergüenza!**
   How shocking!
   En seguida averigüé dónde estaba
   I found out straight away where it was

Regular spelling changes

The consonants **c, g** and **z** are modified by the addition of certain verb or plural endings and by some suffixes. Most of the cases where this occurs have already been dealt with under the appropriate part of speech, but are summarized here along with other instances not covered elsewhere.

Verbs

The changes set out below occur so that the consonant of the verb stem is always pronounced the same as in the infinitive. For verbs affected by these changes see the list of verbs on p. 81.

INFINITIVE	CHANGE	TENSES AFFECTED
-car	c + e → -que	Present subj., pret. (→1)
-cer, -cir	c + a, o → -za, -zo	Present, pres. subj. (→2)
-gar	g + e, i → -gue	Present subj., pret. (→3)
-guar	gu + e → -güe	Present subj., pret. (→4)
-ger, gir	g + a, o → -ja, jo	Present, pres. subj. (→5)
-guir	gu + a, o → -ga, go	Present, pres. subj. (→6)
-zar	z + e → -ce	Present subj., pret. (→7)

Noun and adjective plurals

SINGULAR		PLURAL
vowel + z	→	-ces (→8)

Nouns and adjectives + suffixes

ENDING	SUFFIX	NEW ENDING
vowel + z +	-cito	-cecito (→9)
-go, -ga +	-ito, illo	-guito/a, guillo/a (→10)
-co, -ca +	-ito, illo	-quito/a, quillo/a (→11)

Adjective absolute superlatives

ENDING	SUPERLATIVE
-co	-quísimo (→12)
-go	-guísimo (→13)
vowel + z	-císimo (→14)

1   **Es inútil que lo busques aquí**
It's no good looking for it here
Saqué dos entradas
I got two tickets

2   **Hace falta que venzas tu miedo**
You must overcome your fear

3   **No creo que lleguemos antes**
I don't think we'll be there any sooner
Ya le pagué
I've already paid her

4   **Averigüé dónde estaba la casa**
I found out where the house was

5   **Cojo el autobús, es más barato**
I take the bus, it's cheaper

6   **¿Sigo?**
Shall I go on?

7   **No permiten que se cruce la frontera**
They don't allow people to cross the border
Nunca simpaticé mucho con él
I never got on very well with him

8	**voz → voces** voice voices **veloz → veloces** quick		**luz → luces** light lights **capaz → capaces** capable	
9	**luz** light	→	**lucecita** little light	
10	**amigo** friend	→	**amiguito** chum	
11	**chico** boy	→	**chiquillo** little boy	
12	**rico** rich	→	**riquísimo** extremely rich	
13	**largo** long	→	**larguísimo** very, very long	
14	**feroz** fierce	→	**ferocísimo** extremely fierce	

A, a	[a]	**J, j**	['xota]	**R, r**	['erre]
B, b	[be]	**K, k**	[ka]	**S, s**	['ese]
C, c	[θe]	**L, l**	['ele]	**T, t**	[te]
Ch, ch	[tʃe]	**Ll, ll**	['eʎe]	**U, u**	[u]
D, d	[de]	**M, m**	['eme]	**V, v**	['uβe]
E, e	[e]	**N, n**	['ene]	**W, w**	['uβe'doble]
F, f	['efe]	**Ñ, ñ**	['eɲe]	**X, x**	['ekis]
G, g	[xe]	**O, o**	[o]	**Y, y**	[i'ɣrjeɣa]
H, h	['atʃe]	**P, p**	[pe]	**Z, z**	['θeta]
I, i	[i]	**Q, q**	[ku]		

- The letters are feminine and you therefore talk of **una a**, or **la a**

- Capital letters are used as in English except for the following:
  - adjectives of nationality

  e.g. una ciudad **alemana** un autor **español**
  a German town a Spanish author

  - languages

  e.g. ¿Habla Vd. **inglés**? Hablan **español** e **italiano**
  Do you speak English? They speak Spanish and
  Italian

  - days of the week:

lunes	Monday
martes	Tuesday
miércoles	Wednesday
jueves	Thursday
viernes	Friday
sábado	Saturday
domingo	Sunday

  - months of the year:

enero	January	**julio**	July
febrero	February	**agosto**	August
marzo	March	**se(p)tiembre**	September
abril	April	**octubre**	October
mayo	May	**noviembre**	November
junio	June	**diciembre**	December

Spanish punctuation differs from English in the following ways:

- **Question marks**
  There are inverted question marks and exclamation marks at the beginning of a question or exclamation, as well as upright ones at the end

- **Indications of dialogue**
  Dashes are used to indicate dialogue, and are equivalent to the English inverted commas:
  — ¿Vendrás conmigo? — le preguntó María
  'Will you come with me?' Maria asked him
  Note, however, that when no expression of saying, replying etc. follows, only one dash is used at the beginning:
  — Sí. 'Yes'.

- **Letter headings**
  At the beginning of a letter, a colon is used instead of the English comma:
  Querida Cristina: Dear Cristina,   **Muy Sr. mío:** Dear Sir,

Punctuation terms in Spanish

.	punto	!	se cierra admiración
,	coma	" "	comillas (used as '...')
;	punto y coma	"	se abren comillas
:	dos puntos	"	se cierran comillas
...	puntos suspensivos	( )	paréntesis
¿ ?	interrogación	(	se abre paréntesis
¿	se abre interrogación	)	se cierra paréntesis
?	se cierra interrogación	—	guión
¡ !	admiración		
¡	se abre admiración	punto y aparte	new paragraph
		punto final	last full stop

Cardinal numbers (one, two, three etc.)

cero	0	setenta	70
uno (un, una)	1	ochenta	80
dos	2	noventa	90
tres	3	cien (ciento)	100
cuatro	4	ciento uno(una)	101
cinco	5	ciento dos	102
seis	6	ciento diez	110
siete	7	ciento cuarenta y dos	142
ocho	8	doscientos(as)	200
nueve	9	doscientos(as) uno(una)	201
diez	10	doscientos(as) dos	202
once	11	trescientos(as)	300
doce	12	cuatrocientos(as)	400
trece	13	quinientos(as)	500
catorce	14	seiscientos(as)	600
quince	15	setecientos(as)	700
dieciséis	16	ochocientos(as)	800
diecisiete	17	novecientos(as)	900
dieciocho	18	mil	1.000
diecinueve	19	mil uno(una)	1.001
veinte	20	mil dos	1.002
veintiuno	21	mil doscientos veinte	1.220
veintidós	22	dos mil	2.000
treinta	30	cien mil	100.000
treinta y uno	31	doscientos(as) mil	200.000
cuarenta	40	un millón	1.000.000
cincuenta	50	dos millones	2.000.000
sesenta	60	un billón	1.000.000.000.000

Fractions

un medio; medio(a)	$\frac{1}{2}$
un tercio	$\frac{1}{3}$
dos tercios	$\frac{2}{3}$
un cuarto	$\frac{1}{4}$
tres cuartos	$\frac{3}{4}$
un quinto	$\frac{1}{5}$
cinco y tres cuartos	$5\frac{3}{4}$

Others

cero coma cinco	0,5
uno coma tres	1,3
(el, un) diez por ciento	10%
dos más/y dos	2 + 2
dos menos dos	2 − 2
dos por dos	2 × 2
dos dividido por dos	2 ÷ 2

Points to note on cardinals

- **uno** drops the **o** before masculine nouns, and the same applies when in compound numerals:
  un libro *1 book*, **treinta y un niños** *31 children*

- 1, 21, 31 etc. and 200, 300, 400 etc. have feminine forms:
  cuarenta y una pesetas *41 pesetas*, **quinientas libras** *£500*

- **ciento** is used before numbers smaller than 100, otherwise **cien** is used:
  ciento cuatro *104* BUT **cien pesetas**
  100 pesetas, **cien mil** *100,000* (see also p. 206)

- **millón** takes **de** before a noun:
  un millón de personas *1,000,000 people*

- **mil** is only found in the plural when meaning *thousands of*:
  miles de solicitantes *thousands of applicants*

- cardinals normally precede ordinals:
  los tres primeros pisos *the first three floors*

- Note that the full stop is used with numbers over one thousand and the comma with decimals i.e. the opposite of English usage.

Continued

Ordinal numbers *(first, second, third etc.)*

primero (primer, primera)	1°,1ª	undécimo(a)	11°,11ª
segundo(a)	2°,2ª	duodécimo(a)	12°,12ª
tercero (tercer, tercera)	3°,3ª	decimotercer(o)(a)	13°,13ª
cuarto(a)	4°,4ª	decimocuarto(a)	14°,14ª
quinto(a)	5°,5ª	decimoquinto(a)	15°,15ª
sexto(a)	6°,6ª	decimosexto(a)	16°,16ª
séptimo(a)	7°,7ª	decimoséptimo(a)	17°,17ª
octavo(a)	8°,8ª	decimoctavo(a)	18°,18ª
noveno(a)	9°,9ª	decimonoveno(a)	19°,19ª
décimo(a)	10°,10ª	vigésimo(a)	20°,20ª

Points to note on ordinals

- They agree in gender and in number with the noun, which they normally precede except with Royal titles:

  la primera vez   Felipe segundo
  the first time   Philip II

- **primero** and **tercero** drop the **o** before a masculine singular noun:

  el primer premio   el tercer día
  the first prize   the third day

- Beyond **décimo** ordinal numbers are rarely used, and they are replaced by the cardinal number placed immediately after the noun:

  el siglo diecisiete   **Alfonso doce**   en el piso trece
  the seventeenth century   Alfonso XII   on the 13th floor
  EXCEPTIONS: vigésimo(a) 20th (but not with Royal titles or centuries)
                    centésimo(a) 100th
                    milésimo(a) 1,000th
                    millonésimo(a) 1,000,000th

Numbers: Other Uses

- collective numbers:

un par	2, a couple
una decena (de personas)	about 10 (people)
una docena (de niños)	(about) a dozen (children)
una quincena (de hombres)	about fifteen (men)
una veintena* (de coches)	about twenty (cars)
un centenar, una centena (de casas)	about a hundred (houses)
cientos/centenares de personas	hundreds of people
un millar (de soldados)	about a thousand (soldiers)
miles/millares de moscas	thousands of flies

*20, 30, 40, 50 can also be converted in the same way.

- measurements:

veinte metros cuadrados	20 square metres
veinte metros cúbicos	20 cubic metres
un puente de cuarenta metros de largo/longitud	a bridge 40 metres long

- distance:

De aquí a Madrid hay 400 km	Madrid is 400 km away
a siete km de aquí	7 km from here

Telephone numbers

Póngame con Madrid, el cuatro, cincuenta y ocho, veintidós, noventa y tres
I would like Madrid 458 22 93

Me da Valencia, el veinte, cincuenta y uno, setenta y tres
Could you get me Valencia 20 51 73

Extensión tres, tres, cinco/trescientos treinta y cinco
Extension number 335

N.B. In Spanish telephone numbers may be read out individually, but more frequently they are broken down into groups of two. They are written in groups of two or three numbers (never four).

The Time

¿Qué hora es?   *What time is it?*
Es ... *(1 o'clock, midnight, noon)* ⎫ *It's ...*
Son las ... *(other times)*   ⎭
Es la una y cuarto   *It's 1.15*
Son las diez menos cinco   *It's 9.55*

00.00	medianoche; las doce (de la noche)	*midnight, twelve o'clock*
00.10	las doce y diez (de la noche)	
00.15	las doce y cuarto	
00.30	las doce y media	
00.45	la una menos cuarto	
01.00	la una (de la madrugada)	*one a.m., one o'clock in the morning*
01.10	la una y diez (de la madrugada)	
02.45	las tres menos cuarto	
07.00	las siete (de la mañana)	
07.50	las ocho menos diez	
12.00	mediodía; las doce (de la mañana)	*noon, twelve o'clock*
13.00	la una (de la tarde)	*one p.m., one o'clock in the afternoon*
19.00	las siete (de la tarde)	*seven p.m., seven o'clock in the evening*
21.00	las nueve (de la noche)	*nine p.m., nine o'clock at night*

N.B. When referring to a timetable, the 24 hour clock is used:
las cuatro cincuenta   4.50
las doce treinta y cinco   12.35

¿A qué hora vas a venir? — A las siete
What time are you coming? — At seven o'clock

Las oficinas cierran de dos a cuatro
The offices are closed from two until four

Vendré a eso de/hacia las siete y media
I'll come at around 7.30

a las seis y pico
just after 6 o'clock

a las cinco en punto
at 5 o'clock sharp

entre las ocho y las nueve
between 8 and 9 o'clock

Son más de las tres y media
It's after half past three

Hay que estar allí lo más tarde a las diez
You have to be there by ten o'clock at the latest

Tiene para media hora
He'll be half an hour (at it)

Estuvo sin conocimiento durante un cuarto de hora
She was unconscious for a quarter of an hour

Les estoy esperando desde hace una hora/desde las dos
I've been waiting for them for an hour/since two o'clock

Se fueron hace unos minutos
They left a few minutes ago

Lo hice en veinte minutos
I did it in twenty minutes

El tren llega dentro de una hora
The train arrives in an hour('s time)

¿Cuánto (tiempo) dura la película?
How long does the film last?

por la mañana/tarde/noche
in the morning/afternoon or evening/at night

mañana por la mañana	**ayer por la tarde**
tomorrow morning	yesterday afternoon or evening
anoche **anteayer**	**pasado mañana**
last night the day before yesterday	the day after tomorrow

Dates

¿Qué día es hoy?	} What's the date today?
¿A qué día estamos?	
Es (el) . . .	} It's the . . .
Estamos a . . .	
uno/primero de mayo	1st of May
dos de mayo	2nd of May
veintiocho de mayo	28th of May
lunes tres de octubre	Monday the 3rd of October
Vienen el siete de marzo	They're coming on the 7th of March

N.B. Use cardinal numbers for dates. Only for the first of the month can the ordinal number sometimes be used.

Years

Nací en 1952
I was born in 1952
el tres de octubre de mil novecientos cincuenta y dos
(on) 3rd October 1952

Other expressions

en los años cincuenta	during the fifties
en el siglo veinte	in the twentieth century
en mayo	in May
lunes (quince)	Monday (the 15th)
el quince de marzo	on March the 15th
el/los lunes	on Monday/Mondays
dentro de diez días	in 10 days' time
hace diez días	10 days ago

Age

¿Qué edad tiene?	} How old is he/she?
¿Cuántos años tiene?	
Tiene 23 (años)	He/She is 23
Tiene unos 40 años	He/She is around 40
A los 21 años	At the age of 21

The following index lists comprehensively both grammatical terms and key words in English and Spanish.

COLLINS
GEM
Also available

SPANISH
DICTIONARY

* Over 40,000 references
* Pronunciations clearly shown
* Thousands of current phrases
and constructions

Estoy listo - (I'm ready)
Estoy cansada (" tired)
Tengo hambre / sed
       hungry / thirsty

No sé. (I don't know)
Puede decirme, (Can you tell me)
Puede enseñarme (Can you show me)

a la derecha - to the right

a la izquierda - to the left.

Puedes repetir despacio por favor?

No me siento bien.

Qué bueno es estar de vacaciones

Qué es esto? (this)
Qué es eso? (that)

Qué significa eso?
(What does it mean)

No entiendo.
Me entiende - Do you understand

Es todo - that's all.

Hacer la cama.
To make the bed.

Creo que si - I think so.

Me parece bien.
It seems all right to me.

Sano y salvo - Sound & Safe

Voy a echarle de menos.
I'm going to miss you.

Ir de compras - to go shopping

El ejercicio hace al maestro
Practice makes perfect.

Quedar en casa.
To remain at home.

Mucho gusto en
conocerlo (la)
  (Pleased to meet you)

Mucho gusto - (a pleasure)

El gusto es mio -
(The pleasure is mine)

Buen apetito (Bon appétit)
Buena suerte (Good luck)

Hubimos un buen viaje.
(We had a good trip)

De nada (You're welcome)
Don't complain (No te quejes)
Turn here (Dobla aqui)
There was - Hubo
cucaracha - cockroach